FAITH IN EXILE

*Seeking Hope in
Times of Doubt*

D1316893

JOSEPH T. KELLEY

PAULIST PRESS
New York/Mahwah, N.J.

Scriptural quotations are from the NRSV. Quotations from *The Confessions,* translated by Maria Boulding, O.S.B., are from *The Works of St. Augustine: A Translation for the 21st Century,* copyright © by Augustinian Heritage Institute, New City Press, 1997. Used by permission.

Cover design by Valerie L. Petro / Book design by Joseph E. Petta

Library of Congress Cataloging-in-Publication Data

Kelley, Joseph T., 1948–
    Faith in exile : seeking hope in times of doubt / Joseph T. Kelley.
      p. cm.
    ISBN 0-8091-4088-8
    1. Spiritual life. 2. Meditations. I. Title.
BL624.2 .K45 2003
248.4—dc21

                                     2002006346

Published by Paulist Press
997 Macarthur Boulevard
Mahwah, New Jersey 07430

www.paulistpress.com

Printed and bound in the
United States of America

CONTENTS

For Urszula and Kazimierz Rudnicki,
displaced from earth to heaven,
but too soon.

Acknowledgments

I intentionally avoided footnotes throughout the book for the reader's ease and accessibility to the ideas. So many thinkers of much greater import would find their influence in these pages. I mention specifically Mircea Eliade, Rosemary Haughton, William James, C. S. Lewis, Heinz Kohut, Bernard Lonergan, Alice Miller, John Henry Newman, Rudolph Otto, Karl Rahner, and Houston Smith. Their writings have contributed much to my own intellectual, moral, and spiritual growth and conversions. The immense and varied thought of Saint Augustine continues to enrich me in a multitude of ways.

My own spiritual life and pilgrimage have been greatly blessed by many friends, mentors, and teachers. Some of their ideas and inspiration have filled these pages. I thank them here at the end of this particular part of the journey. My teacher Elie Wiesel brought the scriptural theme of exile alive in new and different ways, and his great compassion brought us much healing. Benedictine monk Kevin Seasoltz of St. John's Abbey lectured many years ago on death and resurrection. Over the years his words have formed and shaped my own difficult times, and helped me always come through to new and fuller life. The Augustinian friars Michael Scanlon, John Rotelle, John Deegan, and Donald Burt of the Villanova Province, together with Frs. Charles Curran of Southern Methodist University and Paul Keyes of St. Michael's parish in North Andover have all been conversation companions over many years on the subjects of grace, sin, and salvation. A day in their house is worth a thousand elsewhere. My colleagues and friends in the Augustinian communities in Massachusetts and in San

Gimignano, Italy, are dear and true spiritual friends, especially James Wenzel and Brian Lowery.

My wife Alina, daughter Kasia, and son Patryk have been very supportive, even when writing has kept me from them. I also wish to thank my friends and colleagues Richard Santagati, Kay DeBurro, Maryanne Reilly, Casey Coburn, Karen Smith, Padraic O'Hare, and Ron Lee for their support and comments. Rev. Lawrence Boadt and Christopher Bellitto of Paulist Press have especially helped to shape and improve the text.

Finally there are my own students at Merrimack College over many years, especially the continuing education students whose life experiences and healthy skepticism of easy academic answers helped to shape my own language and thought. Their companionship in the classroom, their willingness to speak about their own spiritual pilgrimages and religious exiles, and their openness to new life, to *chai,* continues to be a source of great hope.

Joseph T. Kelley
Merrimack College
August 28, 2001

Introduction

Many people today feel alienated from religion. There are various reasons for this alienation. A once-faithful believer may have drifted away slowly and unawares until lost in uncharted seas of doubt. Another may have set sail intentionally into unfamiliar waters of religious questioning and agnosticism. Still others may have been cast into troubled seas by the religious piracy of someone who should have been trustworthy.

For the religiously displaced, by any means or for any reason, these pages extend a gentle invitation to plot one's current position. Like pilots' charts, arranged and waiting on the bridge, these chapters may help you to get a reading on where you have dropped anchor, to take some depth soundings of what lies beneath, to study the stars above by night, to scan the horizon by day for the possibility of eventual landfall and some sure footing. These pages do not necessarily point in one direction or another with religious certainty. A return to one's original religion, or conversion to a new faith, may or may not be in the stars. For some people, religious answers and convictions always seem just over the distant horizon, receding as one approaches.

This book may, however, help you find enough certitude to continue the spiritual passage toward the horizon or the shore that holds the most hope for you. There is one conviction in these pages that I trust the careful reader will come to share. That is the confidence that no matter where one might find oneself regarding institutional religion, it is possible to have a spiritual life. In fact, the spiritual life is what fills our sails and moves us across the sea of life in search of some religious port or other. Without a spiritual life, our vessel of faith sits deadly still and, like the ancient mariner, we can lose all hope.

The understanding of spirituality here is a simple one. Spirituality is one's relationship with God, with the Holy One, with that which is transcendent to all human experience and to all creation. To live a spiritual life is to reflect on this relationship and to work it gently into the warp and woof of daily life in meaningful patterns. The faithful member of a congregation can enjoy a deep, abiding, and thoughtful relationship with God. Likewise, someone who feels religiously displaced, who may be alienated from institutional religion, can also have a meaningful relationship with God, be intentional about it, and make it part of daily life. Spirituality and the spiritual life are nobody's and no group's monopolies. The spirit of God moves when and where it will.

The pages that follow are written for devout believers as well as for the skeptics who keep a comfortable distance from religion, for those who struggle with their faith and for those who struggle because of their faith. There are no formulas, no meditation techniques, no esoteric teachings here to enrich one's spiritual life, though such things may be of great help at times. Rather, three basic themes are brought forward to enhance spiritual reflection and practice. These three themes are place, diligence, and hope.

Place reminds us that the spiritual life is not really so mysterious and otherworldly. It happens here among human beings like you and me. It takes place, that is, it takes its place in our lives along with many other human experiences. We have to accommodate spirituality, to account for its place and give it space in our lives. It does not magically defy space and time, though it can mysteriously transform them.

The second theme is diligence. The spiritual life is also the diligent life. Not diligence in the word's more rigorous meaning of paying meticulous attention to details. Rather, diligence in the original and root meaning of loving care. Diligence is the virtue of loving care for oneself, for others, and for the world. As such, diligence is the cardinal virtue of the spiritual life.

The third and final theme is hope. Spiritual experience and the spiritual life can be tested for their authenticity by asking how much hope they inspire. Hope is diligent anticipation of the future. Hope is realized by the loving care we devote to our own growth and development, by the diligent attention we give to the unfolding potential of others, and by our dedication to the promise that the world holds. Hope is not simple optimism, blind to the pain and doubt of life, even of the spiritual life. Hope is a choice to affirm the possibilities that life in general and the spiritual life in particular hold for ourselves, for others, and for the world we share.

These meditations on place, diligence, and hope are largely inspired and generally informed by Christian theology, for that has been my own soul craft. However, such theology is in its best moments open, hospitable, and accessible to all persons of good will and spiritual yearning; it can help shed light on our common human experience and on the ultimate meaning of life. That at least is my hope. Whether one is a committed Christian, a displaced believer, a struggling agnostic, or some combination thereof, thoughtful reflection can enrich one's spiritual life. Devout or displaced believers from other religious traditions will also know that making space for spirituality in one's life, developing diligence, and deepening hope are not only Christian virtues. They are fundamental categories found in many spiritual traditions. Indeed, one might say they are moral imperatives for our shared life on this Earth.

A discussion about place, diligence, and hope is therefore a good meeting place, a safe harbor where spiritual travelers from a great variety of convictions or of doubts can put in. Conversation about the role of these three virtues in the spiritual life can provide some mooring for our barks, some anchorage for our anxieties. They offer us the opportunity to meet on the shore and share stories about our spiritual journeys, about the places we have been, and about where we hope to go.

PART ONE

Place:
Suffering the Sense of Religious Exile

Where can I go from your spirit?
Or where can I flee from your presence?
If I ascend to heaven, you are there.
If I make my bed in Sheol, you are there.
If I take the wings of the morning
And settle at the farthest limits of the sea,
Even there your hand shall lead me,
Your right hand shall hold me fast.
Psalm 139:7–10

CHAPTER 1

Sacred Space

I f you were to travel across the Indian subcontinent, as my father did many years ago, your journey would take you through hundreds or even thousands of villages. Almost every village you visit would have its own local god or goddess, its "avatar" or particular piece of revealed divinity. For the Hindu believer, the transcendent is reflected and refracted in a million different splashes of local color, each emerging from its own nook or cranny among the valleys, plains, and majestic mountains of this great and ancient land. You would see that the people in each village treasure their particular revelation. This divinity is their special and distinct connection with the one that is above all, revealed in a particular way in this particular place.

A glance at the history of religions shows that, like India, many ancient cultures had divinities or demons that were very much associated with particular places. In pre-Christian Ireland, for example, a powerful spirit might be thought to dwell in or around this rock or that tree. Passing under the tree or close to the rock meant approaching that spirit's turf and quite possibly incurring its wrath. One had to learn and to remember where spirits lived, and then to treat that place with respect and awe. Such places often marked the territories of rival clans and kings who lived under the protection of their local supernatural supervisor.

In the ancient Mideast, as well, divinities were believed to take up residence in locales over which they ruled. Gods and goddesses homesteaded here or there, and claimed that land for themselves. Travel was dangerous for the roving clan or caravan. For if you did not know which particular divine real estate you had happened upon, and what ritual toll was expected, you might suffer unfortunate consequences. The earliest levels of biblical texts are filled with the exotic names and markers of these local spots, such as Beer-lahai-roi and Beer-sheba, where patriarchs and priests encountered the divine. Later Judaic religion continued to cherish these sacred places and to associate them in biblical stories with the gradual revelation of the Holy One, Yahweh.

The great cathedrals of medieval European Christianity, sometimes built on pre-Christian sanctuaries, mark a high point of sacred placing. Their architecture and art are grand elaborations of this persistent phenomenon of particular meeting places between the human and the divine. Their towers and spires express the sacred exchange between heaven and earth. Their hallowed stone altars ground these great churches in the earth, and connect them to the simpler haunted rocks of long-ago tribal religions. Their stained glass catches, suffuses, and scatters the same piercing light that once dazzled shamans and sorcerers who came to that place for a prayer or a vision.

This ancient practice of recognizing the holiness of special sites is not just a curiosity of the past. Believers of many faiths continue to hold certain places sacred. Particular rivers or rocks, grottos or mountains, churches or temples are still visited by prayerful pilgrims because worshipers sense the divine presence there in some special way. These are holy spots, and believers feel they are in the presence of the divine when they approach the environs. So each year millions make the journey to Lourdes, to Mecca, to Rome, to the Ganges, to Buddh Gaya, to Jerusalem, and to a thousand other such places where they hope to stand on hallowed land or enter sacred precincts.

Such places may indeed have something to do with a divine predilection for the particular. On the human side of the equation, however, this curious habit of associating divinity or sanctity with particular places reveals something significant about us. We might find God especially here, or grace particularly there, because a sense of place is so important and essential for us, and for our spiritual life.

Sacred Times

Ancient religions had not only sacred places where one could enter into holy commerce with the transcendent, they also had appointed times for such sacred interchange. The turn of a season, such as spring planting or fall harvest, the midwinter or midsummer solstice, or an annual holy day of remembrance all helped to set sacred times and to hail holy celebrations for tribal traditions. Such times would be marked by fasting and feasting, by religiousness and revelry, by excess and recess.

One such time of celebration and sacred encounter was the beginning of each new year. Different tribes would observe the beginning of the year in their particular culture at different seasons. For some, like the ancient Hebrews, the year began in the fall, around the harvest festival. For others, the year would begin with the winter solstice, the day when sunlight stopped diminishing and began to increase, however imperceptibly. For still others, the springtime signaled new beginnings as life returned to the earth. At all such observances of annual renewals, tribal and ancient peoples believed that the world once again intersected with its divine beginnings. The creator, however understood or imaged by a people, would exercise the divine prerogative once more and keep the cycle of life turning. It was always a sacred and frightful moment, surrounded by special rituals to protect and ensure the continuity of creation.

Another kind of sacred moment in ancient religion was that which surrounded important events in the life of the community. Birth, coming of age, marriage, illness, and death might each have its own ritual to mark the passage from one stage of life to another. Sometimes these were community celebrations, when members of the tribe would join together in celebration. At other times rites of passage were to be made alone. In all cases the hours, days, or weeks proscribed and allotted for the commemoration and celebration were sacred moments, when time was transformed by the powers or spirits that entered it, and souls were seared by the supernatural.

Contemporary religions also observe sacred times that provide opportunities for reflection and remembrance. These liturgical or holy times mark certain days or weeks as having special meaning and as affording special grace. Rosh Hashanah, the celebration of the New Year, and nine days later Yom Kippur, the Day of Atonement, are the holiest time in the Jewish calendar, time set aside to observe endings and to rejoice in fresh beginnings. Each Sabbath is a day for resting with God. Advent and Christmas, Lent and Easter provide Christians with annual opportunities for spiritual renewal, for remembrance of Jesus' birth, death, and resurrection, and for joyful expectation about the future. Each Sunday is the Lord's Day. Ramadan is the holy time of fasting and prayer each year for Muslims. Each day of this holy month is sanctified by fasting until sunset, and by special attention to the times of daily prayer. And every Friday is for intensified devotion.

Not only seasons and days, but hours of the day can have sacred power and significance. For Jews sundown is sacred, holding in its embrace the beginnings of a new day and the new Sabbath. For Muslims every day is sanctified by the five hours of prayer, each begun by ritual washing and marked by gestures of submission to Allah. For Christians, morning, noon, evening, and the night vigil have their proper liturgical hours of prayer to recall God's loving power and presence in human history.

Your Own Sacred Places and Times

To begin the spiritual life, or return to it, we need to allot it time and space. Ancient peoples had their holy days and their haunted spots. The great world religions of today treasure their sacred shrines and observe holy seasons. If we wish to experience the spiritual life, we too must discover places and times that are holy and sacred for us personally. We need to replicate on a very personal level the age-old religious practice of sacred spots and hallowed moments. We must discern precincts and seasons that enrich and advance our spirituality. We need to locate these places, identify these times, and covet them. While spirituality by definition deals with spirit, it is an incarnate paradox that our spiritual lives need real time and real space in order to flourish. Talking about spirituality is not the same as living it. And living it begins with giving it time and space in our otherwise busy lives.

Where are these personal sacred places? For some it might be the house of religious worship in their own religious tradition, a favorite church or synagogue, a particular mosque or monastery. Such conventional sacred places in our own religious heritage can hold special power and significance that opens our minds and hearts to God. Others will perhaps discover that a sacred place in another religious tradition can be surprisingly effective in unlocking their spiritual lives. The Christian monk Thomas Merton recounted how, before his conversion, he would stop in a New York City church simply to watch and marvel at the sight of people in silent prayer. Merton's experience of observing people at prayer in their sacred place opened the future monk up to the possibility of his own spiritual life. In similar ways we can often discover a fresh and even astonishing new avenue to our souls by glimpsing how other faiths or traditions invite their faithful to spirituality.

For still others, their personal sacred place may be found not in a religious building, but in nature. It may be mountains they have grown to know and love, or stretches of familiar beach, or the vast openness and silent emptiness of the great plains. It may be a certain lake or river, city or village, or even a specific region or country. It may be the endless expanse of the night sky inviting one into the immensity of the universe itself.

Just as we can locate places or spaces in our lives that call us to the spiritual life, we can do the same with time. People who joke about being a "morning person" or a "night owl" refer to their ability to function better at one time of the day rather than another. Just so, there are times of the day when we are able to be more reflective. It may be early in the morning, before we begin the day's tasks, or midday, when we feel the need to retreat temporarily from our responsibilities. For others the evening is a better time to stop, with the day's work accomplished, and then to reflect. There are even those for whom the quiet, undisturbed hours of night and the stillness of pre-dawn are the most fruitful for the soul. There are also times associated with certain tasks— time spent cooking, putting a child to bed or rocking her to sleep, wrapping a gift, taking photographs, reading poetry, waiting for the return of a loved one—any time might be particularly sacred for a person because of the inherent call to reflection that it extends.

Certain times of the year also provide us with their own natural invitations to spirituality. Reflecting the moods of nature, we may respond to a certain season that both refreshes our soul and draws us within ourselves. Other days or months may carry a great deal of meaning because they mark the anniversaries of births, or recall memories of departed loved ones, or hark back to significant events in our life. They draw us naturally into reflective moods, sometimes marked by pain, sometimes by joy. These particular times and seasons are not only dates to mark on the kitchen calendar. They are also invitations to our souls.

It is not always easy to discern where one's own personal sacred place might be, and when's best to visit it. The advantage of organized religions and their long traditions is that appointed times and established places are handed down with centuries of religious practice and devotion. How do we possibly discern sacredness among the more mundane times and places of our daily life? How do we know what particular spaces in our own immediate world might foster awareness of grace or open us to the presence of the holy? It takes intention and attention to identify, to claim, and then to visit one's personal sacred times and places. After all, believers attest that the Virgin Mary chose Lourdes and Mohammed Mecca. For the Jewish faithful, Passover has been sanctified and sanctifying for over three millennia. Buddha chose the very spot to sit and meditate until he reached nirvana. Jesus was born in Bethlehem and died in Jerusalem and rose from the dead in three days. How do we claim those special places in our own familiar territory that we might dare call sacred? How do we mark in our calendars those weeks or days or hours that might be somehow holy for us?

Sacred Interiority

Perhaps the most important characteristic of our own personal sacred times and places is their ability to draw us within ourselves. If we identify certain spots or moments in our ambit of life as sacred, it is because they somehow encourage or invite us to go within and visit our soul. They induce us to know and experience who we are in the deepest, most fundamental ways of being a person. They provide ways, unique and peculiar to each of us, that express and reveal, unlock or elicit our inner life. They introduce, or reintroduce us to our deeper self. They mirror on the outside that place inside us where we touch God, or where God touches us. They provide opportunities for encounter with God, because they first offer us a gentle invitation to encounter and enter our own self. Our personal sacred places and times are holy because they are invitations to interiority.

Many of the ancient, tribal holy places were located either in caves or on mountaintops. Such places can be understood both to symbolize and to invite an encounter with the interior self. The spiritual wayfarer would enter a sacred cave as a way of expressing and effecting the journey within. The sacred mountain afforded the pilgrim a new and arresting perspective, a climb to clear sight of where one had come from in life and where one might be going. In a similar way, by entering our personal sacred space, we step aside the daily roads and highways of life. There, in our own kind of cave or from our personal summit, we encounter our more authentic self, that part of us that ordinarily remains hidden and buried, or distant and out of sight. These special spaces, because of the unique perspective they afford, liberate us. They free us from the everyday demands put upon us by others, by society, even by ourselves. There we can see and listen in ways not afforded by the ordinary.

Sacred times can also be invitations to interiority. Quiet moments that catch us and call us within are holy opportunities. They may come unbidden, or we can work them intentionally into our lives as ways of keeping in touch with our self. Certain events also provide us occasions to remember and reflect on the inner life. Special celebrations, such as weddings, births, or anniversaries, not only mark new beginnings and the passing of years. They also manifest the life of the soul. The vibrancy and potential of our inner self is stirred by such special times when we rejoice in nature's gifts or honor human choices. Such observances also mark limit and boundary; they recall beginnings, celebrate cycles, and mark endings. As such they can mirror our deep inner experiences of limit and boundary. Such times can recall the finiteness of our own existence, of our knowledge, of our ability. Limit or boundary moments plunge us into our nature as creatures.

There are many combinations of times and places that open up a great variety of ways into our deeper selves. These roads to interiority are also paths to the sacred. The deeper we go into ourselves, the closer we come to the holy. The times and places that afford us opportunities to dwell in our more authentic selves are also occasions of grace, inviting us into the presence of the divine mystery within.

Pilgrimage: The Rhythm of the Spiritual Life

Another glance at the history of religions shows that people in search of the divine would make pilgrimages. A pilgrimage is a combination of sacred space and sacred time. At a certain time or season of the year deemed holy by a culture or a religion, the pilgrims would set off on a journey to a holy place in hopes of encountering the holy.

The great religions of Western civilization are famous for their holy journeys. For millennia Jews have sought to celebrate Passover in Jerusalem, choosing the holy days as the time to visit this most sacred of all cities. Muslims hope, at least once during their lifetime, to make the *hegira* and visit Mecca, preferably during Ramadan. Christians had been crisscrossing Europe for centuries on pilgrimage to their sacred shrines even long before Chaucer's characters set out for Canterbury. In the East, Hindus have for millennia been making the long and often difficult journey to bathe in the Ganges. Buddhists revere and visit the site of Buddha's own time of enlightenment at Buddh Gaya, where he sat under the Bodhi tree for forty-nine days.

A first step in the spiritual life is to identify one's own sacred place or places, and to discern what times or seasons are most favorable for interiority. Then we can, in our own personal ways, combine our sacred places and our sacred times to form our own little personal pilgrimages. These personal pilgrimages can be taken daily, weekly, monthly, or in some combination. For some people it will be important to visit their sacred place once a day at a time that is most helpful to them. It might be for only a few moments, but these few moments can work to keep them rooted and centered in their interior life for the whole day. If the personal pilgrimage is made in the morning, memories of it can pervade and enrich the rest of the day. If it is made later in the day, anticipation can fill the day with new purpose and meaning. If it is the stillness of the night that calls one to personal pilgrimage, the serenity of the dark hours can calm and quiet the busy hours of the day.

Some will find a special pilgrimage every week or so provides extra nourishment and strength for the soul. A seasonal retreat or annual pilgrimage may also be supportive for the interior life. A certain time of the year calls some people to spend days for and with themselves in a place that is away from the daily hubbub. This retreat from ordinary life becomes a powerful event in their lives, enriching the rest of the year. Whatever our own pattern or preference, we need to make those personal pilgrimages so that the spiritual life becomes a real part of us. We need to know what places resonate with our inner selves, and what times echo the songs in our souls. We need to take account of such times and places, and choose to enter them willingly and attentively, for they help us to honor, cherish, and reflect upon our inner life. Making personal pilgrimages is a way to begin the journey of the spiritual life.

It is not, however, an easy thing for people, especially those of us in Western cultures, to find places that are sacred for us, nor is it easy to find times that open up ways into the soul. We are so busy, so beset. We tend to think about place and time as commodities that can make us money, rather than as opportunities that can take us within. We measure and divide land to make it ever more marketable and functional. Space is sold, bought, rented, leased, assigned, and foreclosed on. We suffer the loss of more and more shared, public space, such as the town or city square, and the growth of more and more privately owned spaces, such as malls and gated communities. We roam through the corporately owned corridors of massive malls where private property law applies and social order is determined by the marketing of goods rather than by the common good.

We also consider time as a commodity. We spend it, earn it, lose it, gain it, accumulate it, and eventually run out of it. We quantify time, measuring it in ever smaller units, useful perhaps for science and technology, but overused in life. We sacrifice each day in its measured pieces apportioned for the ancient Greek god Chronos as we go about synchronizing our lives and our selves with his relentless tick.

Of course we must negotiate our way in the world by using space and spending time. Spirituality does not mean we dismiss practicality. The difficulty for us in contemporary Western culture, however, is that our social and economic structures distract or preclude us from the deeper meanings and possibilities in time and space. At our hurried pace we rush by the many personal sacred sanctuaries that could soothe our souls. Under the pressure of time we miss the private moments that proffer inner peace and quiet. We are encouraged by advertisements and commercials to stop at the surface, discouraged from delving within.

In most religious traditions pilgrims walk, marking their journey step by step, taking their time, reaching their goal by modest daily increments. Few choices could be so countercultural, so contradictory to life in our fast-paced information age, as to set out on such a slow, difficult, and deliberate journey. Those who wish to live the spiritual life must also go against the cultural grain. This does not necessarily mean that we all have to set out on a long, holy trek to a distant shrine. Yet, to discern for ourselves what daily times and familiar places help us enter the near yet distant sanctuary of our souls will be to do something quite different from the cultural norm, quite alternative to society's dictates. To make those short and simple everyday pilgrimages to our own personal holy place, in our own sacred time, takes some doing. To put aside time and set off space for our souls is not a skill we are taught or tutored in. Yet it is the first step of the spiritual journey.

Choose to Start

To make a pilgrimage requires decision. A pilgrim does not wander haphazardly, but sets out and moves along with intention and dedication. Yet a pilgrimage is also not a forced march, relentlessly coerced and compelled by guilt or fear. Pilgrimage is an adventure, a journey of discovery. Like the varied characters of *The Canterbury Tales,* whom we come to know like traveling companions in reading Chaucer, our personal pilgrimage will time by time and place by place slowly reveal more and more about the many dimensions of our own character, about who we are in the deeper parts of our selves. The diligent observance of our personal sacred times and places also offers the opportunity to know more about the divine character, and about God's ever-diligent, ever-faithful presence along the pilgrim way.

Start your pilgrimage simply and slowly. Do not complicate it. Identify and choose your sacred times, your sacred places. Then weave them into your life in regular patterns as well as creative variations. If you begin to wander away off the pilgrim path, don't fret. Simply find your way back, as best you can, to those places and times that nourish and refresh the soul. There you will find strength for the journey.

Certainly, for most of us there will be detours on our pilgrimage, as well as cul-de-sacs, false starts, and some trails that disappear in the underbrush. Indeed, as we shall see, our pilgrimage may lead us into exile, into deserted places and unseasonable times that feel far from sacred or holy. We may be displaced by circumstance, distracted from our intentions, distressed in our souls. The spiritual pilgrimage lasts a lifetime and will take us over many roads we could never have imagined at the beginning. Some of those roads will be difficult and discouraging. Always, to begin or to continue the journey, the pilgrim needs only to observe those times and cherish those places that keep one in touch with the soul. To return there constantly, with diligence and hope, without blame or shame, is to live the pilgrim life.

There are other ways to the sacred. Good works, the faithful observance of religious customs and prayers, and the study of philosophy and theology are all paths that can lead a person to deeper and deeper experiences of or encounter with the sacred. Sooner or later, however, each of these paths must intersect with the way of interiority. By whatever road one travels through life toward the sacred and holy, that road will eventually merge with the way of interiority, for our primary encounter with the sacred is through our souls, through what is deepest within us. It is there, in the depths of our selves, that we come face to face with what is beyond our selves, beyond our being. There we touch Being itself.

If we do develop the habit of making our personal pilgrimages, the practice will in time have distinct effects on us. As we identify and visit our own sacred places, as we recognize and observe our own sacred times, we slowly, eventually become habituated to the sacred. We begin to discover the sacred at other times, in other places where we had never thought to look. In this way more and more opportunities to make personal pilgrimages present themselves. Because we, as faithful pilgrims, discover more and more occasions to go within our souls, and more and more places where the transcendent seems to break through to us, our spiritual lives build and build. The so-called secular becomes sanctified. The ordinary becomes replete with the extraordinary. All of life gradually is transformed into a pilgrimage.

We begin to discover that all time and space is sacred, filled with transcendent possibility. By frequent and regular visits to those places that open us up to our interior life, we begin to live consistently out of the deeper, more authentic parts of ourselves no matter where we might be. By seizing those times that call us within, we gradually understand that all time is an invitation, an opportunity, to transform the moment by living it from the very depths of our soul. By treasuring those times and places that provide us with precious interiority, we can discover that every place is a point of intersection with the sacred, that God is embedded in every moment, that all time and every place is the province of God's infinite love.

CHAPTER 2

Exile

We enter the spiritual life by times and places that are holy. Our spiritual pilgrimages bring us through sacred space into the sanctuary of our souls. Yet the spiritual life can just as often be a matter of losing one's place, of getting displaced. Spiritual pilgrimage can become a journey into exile.

Exile is the experience of displacement. People who are exiled have been removed from their rightful place, from home, from country, from where they belong or long to be. There are different kinds of exile. There are exiles that result from political or social forces. Or one can suffer personal exile because of broken relationships and violations of trust. There is also religious exile, when a person has been displaced from his or her religious background or upbringing. One may have left or been forced out of the faith community that has been one's religious home, one's religious place.

We can also speak of spiritual exile. This is not just removal from a religious tradition or the forsaking of a church. It is more. It is alienation from God, a profound feeling of abandonment by the Holy One. This spiritual exile can infect the other kinds of exile and deepen their already painful effects.

Exile in the Bible

One could write much of human history by chronicling the forced displacement of tribes and nations. In fact, much of biblical history is written just this way. Bible stories rise and subside on the ebb and flow of displacement, of exile and return. The very first biblical drama is a tragedy that climaxes in the original human exile. Adam and Eve must leave Eden, displaced by pride from their rightful, given place, a sacred garden where they had enjoyed free and unquestioned access to God. Eden was the first sacred place, the original holy spot, the archetype for every later sacred plot or tree or rock or mountain that would multiply around the Earth with the spread of the human family. And it was lost.

In the land of the first human exile, east of Eden, the tragic story of displacement continues. Cain kills his brother Abel, "displaces" him to death, and is then condemned to wander alone and forsaken. Cain bears the brand of an exile on his forehead, to be identified and recognized by humanity forever as the first exiled murderer, displaced from human contact by his crime.

As the Book of Genesis continues, biblical stories about the ancestors of the Hebrews continue to tell of displacement. The elder Abraham travels to a foreign land, displaced from his home of many years by God's call and his own faithful response. Abraham's grandson Jacob also spends many years living in exile, displaced to a distant land by his love and desire to wed Rachel. When Jacob has finally won Rachel, he returns to the land of his father, Isaac. Then it is his wife who must leave her home: Rachel, who symbolizes the millions of women displaced over the millennia by marriage, grafted onto the tribe and clan of their husbands, expected to take root in a new and strange soil.

Jacob's favorite son Joseph is sold into exile by his jealous brothers, who are themselves later displaced to Egypt by famine. When all the sons of Jacob are in Egypt, the emerging Hebrew people begin their five hundred years of exile, removed from the land promised to Abraham. Even after Moses leads the people out of Egypt into freedom, they suffer another exile. The very redemption of Israel out of slavery means another displacement in the desert of Sinai, one that lasts for a whole generation. Moses himself dies in exile, in sight of the Promised Land, but unable to enter.

Seven hundred years after the Hebrews had returned to Israel, they are exiled to Babylon, displaced once again from their cherished ancestral land. Finally, when Rome destroys Jerusalem, the inhabitants are dispersed and the great Galut or wandering of Jews begins and lasts for two thousand years. The stories of the Hebrew scriptures are so many painful variations on the themes of religious, political, and social displacement. From the banishment of Adam and Eve to the Roman destruction of Jerusalem, God's chosen people become experts in exile.

Even the Christian New Testament's proclamation of "good news" begins with stories that involve displacement. The census ordered by Caesar Augustus required everyone to travel back to his ancestral town. At the time of Jesus' birth his parents were in a strange town with no lodging, displaced by political officialdom and its machinery. The magi, far from their own kingdoms in the East, are in a kind of self-imposed exile, displaced by their own star-struck search for a savior. Soon the child Jesus and his parents, threatened by the political conniving of Herod, are forced to retrace the exile of their ancestors and are displaced like the Hebrews of old to Egypt. So much of biblical history is the story of leaving or being forced to leave, of wandering and wondering, of banishment and exile, of displacement.

Personal Exile

The biblical themes of exile are echoed today in contemporary political displacements and social exiles around the world. However, they also resonate in the daily displacements suffered by individuals and families. These personal exiles may be less epic, but they are no less real. Though not of biblical proportions, personal exiles are nonetheless distressing and devastating.

When a marriage ends in divorce, a family is thrown into exile. The patterns of family life, reassuring even with their tensions and troubles, are left behind for new and strange places of uncertain rights and rules. Parents and children must often leave the familiarity of home and neighborhood, frequently feeling they carry the mark of Cain, branded and exiled by guilt for the failure of the family. In-laws, relatives, and friends are also displaced by confusion, hurt, and disappointment. Even in cases where the end of a marriage or relationship is the wiser way, those involved suffer an exile from intimacy.

The loss of a job or occupation is another type of exile. People are called into the boss's office to be told they are part of the latest downsizing. Displacement begins. It may be the dirty politics of the workplace or the tyranny of a boss that result in one's separation. Like Joseph, son of Jacob, one may feel betrayed and sold down the pike by close associates, displaced by silver pieces soiling fraternal hands. The loss of work, and of the income, security, and meaning that it provides, leaves one banished and branded.

Serious illness is another type of displacement. When we are sick, we are removed from the ordinary, workaday world that, despite its toils and tests, gives us a sense of place. We can find ourselves expatriate patients, removed from the bustling business and comforting commerce of life. When the diagnosis is a difficult and disturbing one, we may even be exiled from our own future, our hopes, and our dreams. The progression of a disease can leave one feeling exiled from one's own body.

Mental illness and psychological suffering also involve experiences of radical displacement. One who suffers in such ways often feels exiled from his or her own sense of self, expelled from normalcy, deported by inner despots and demons. Neuroses, psychoses, and other disorders can leave one feeling like the Jews who were carted off to Babylon, to exile in a foreign land of unreasonable inner tyrants, a land from which one fears there is no return.

Perhaps the greatest personal exile we suffer, however, is when we lose loved ones in death. They were there, and now they are gone. They have been removed from their familiar place next to us, removed, it seems, from that one place that was most surely theirs: their body. Now they no longer have a "place" at all. Their passing leads us to wonder how strong a grasp we have on our own place in life. When a loved one dies, all life seems so fragile, so fleeting, so easily displaced and disposed of.

Religious Exile

Besides political, social, and personal exile, there is also religious exile, which can be of two types. One type, often a dimension of political or social exile, involves the persecution, forced conversion, or systematic removal of a religious group or community because of their faith. This kind of religious exile is often suffered by a whole population or by an entire community. The lists of offenders and victims fill historical volumes. Such persecution continues to be all too common in the present day; it shows the dark, shadow side of religion.

The second type of religious exile is what concerns us here. It is less political or social, and more of an individual nature. Most people are born into some religious tradition that is part of their family heritage. This religion is part of the place one calls home. However, people can get displaced from that religious heritage. They can suffer some degree of disengagement from the religious place where they started, not because of political misfortune or persecution, but because of their own personal decisions or circumstances.

Sometimes such personal religious displacement is a marked and abrupt response to a specific cause. Betrayal by a religious leader, the hypocrisy of a believer, the official statement or stand of one's church or congregation: any of these can rip a believer out of his or her place of faith and meaning. A child can be displaced, torn from the tenderness of early faith and thrown into confusion and fear by the perfidy of a believer. The physical or sexual abuse of children by a clergy person, teacher, or other religious leader can leave a child emotionally exiled, even if he or she remains physically in the congregation. Verbal and psychological abuse inflicted by a religious leader or propagated by a whole religious community can also leave children, adolescents, and even adults alienated, anxious, and angry.

Other less traumatic but still unfortunate situations can cause people to exile themselves and abandon their religion. A pastor or minister or rabbi may, even without intending it, be the occasion of a person leaving the faith. An unkind word, a lapse of patience, or the failure to respond to someone's pastoral or spiritual need can push a believer into religious exile. Sometimes it is not an individual pastor or minister who is the occasion of exile, but the whole group or institution. It may be the church's stance on a particular issue or the congregation's lack of involvement in certain causes. Consistently poor preaching or uninspired worship services, a lack of support or no sense of community, an ethos of intolerance or perceived hypocrisy can all result in the exile of a believer. Even elderly members of a faith community can, after decades of dedication, find that the sanctuary where they have spent their lives in worship and service has become inhospitable or forbidding.

At other times personal religious exile is less abrupt or sudden. It is more a slow drifting away, almost unnoticed at first. One can gradually lose touch with the religious practices of youth. Religion may have become one of those Waterloos of adolescence where the parent finally lost the battle or the nerve necessary to insist on religious observance. Then, suddenly it seems, one is no longer a rebellious adolescent but a young adult who has ended up, without ever seriously intending it, religiously displaced. One may occasionally return for a friend's wedding or a relative's funeral and find the feeling of displacement palpable. And one is not quite sure how to get re-placed.

Religious exile can also be a result of what might be called "inner displacement." In such instances it is not so much a matter of reacting or responding to a perceived fault in the religion itself or in the congregation, but of slowly accruing inner changes in the mind and heart of the believer. In all areas of our lives, when we grow in knowledge and experience we constantly displace ideas and feelings. The way we understood love at fourteen has been displaced by the way we understand love now—after some considerable experience, no doubt. The way we appreciate our mother or father now has displaced our previous appreciation of them, or lack thereof. The way we practice our profession or craft now is very different from when we first began. Years of work, of trial and error, of growing insight and skill, have displaced our earlier ways of working with our now more mature talent. Previously held convictions about political parties and causes, about ethical values and issues, about former heroes and yesterday's enemies are all displaced as we change and grow and develop.

We are complicit in these intellectual and emotional displacements that we undergo. So long as we continue to grow and change, to think and reconsider, to remain open and curious, we are constantly displacing all sorts of things in our minds and hearts. These inner changes, at least when we are making them, can seem unimportant. Then one day we look back and realize that all these inner displacements have one by one brought us to a whole new place in life. We become displaced, all unawares, by the ways we have changed within ourselves.

These small, quiet, but accumulating displacements can happen in matters of faith. Our growing, changing ideas or experience can slowly take us away from the safe and secure religion of our past. Little by little, day by day, by exercising our own voluntary nature, we can gradually remove ourselves from our faith, as we displace ideas and understandings and affections that characterized our childhood faith.

Such religious displacement can be about doctrine. We can grow inquisitive, even skeptical about God or about official teachings of our faith. Religious convictions, disturbed by quietly growing questions and doubts, may eventually be abandoned and cast off as remnants of childhood. Or, one's religious questions may concern ethical issues and moral problems. Behaviors once thought sinful are no longer judged to be so; believers cannot return to their earlier religious naivete, yet they may feel confused and guilty. They have become exiled from the simpler faith and morals of their childhood.

Sometimes struggling believers may be especially sensitive to what they begin to perceive as their church's or their congregation's spiritual shallowness. Without realizing it, they slowly detect that their religious community has itself been co-opted by the more mediocre mores of the wider culture. They may come to see that their church or its leaders operate out of the uncritical values of a consumer-oriented society. They grow to suspect there is something amiss in the way religious teachings are calcified and canonized to the point that they no longer invite believers into the deeper realities they express and symbolize. Or one can be scandalized by the way some members of the religious community treat other members, especially those with whom they may disagree. So such believers become alienated from their church because of their own perceptiveness, and exiled from religion because of their growing sensitivity to its failings.

Religious displacement, however it has taken root and grown, usually leaves one with all sorts of questions about life, death, God, faith, and morals. The explanations and answers that were once provided by one's faith are no longer satisfactory; they have been displaced. The believer has wandered away, or been driven out of his or her religious tradition, into religious exile.

Spiritual Exile

It is possible that a person may be quite alienated from religion, put out or put off by an experience in the church or congregation, yet still feel connected to God. Such a person may in fact enjoy an active spiritual life and attend to it daily. Though displaced from institutional religion for some reason or other, a believer may feel spiritually well placed and may live an active and vital spiritual life. There is, however, another and deeper kind of alienation or exile. It is spiritual exile, which has less to do with one's relationship with and feelings about religious heritage and tradition. Spiritual exile concerns how one experiences and reflects on relationship with God. If the spiritual life is how relationship with God is perceived and felt, how it affects one's sense of self and one's value and identity, then spiritual exile is a felt loss of that relationship and all it might have offered.

Spiritual exile can happen to anyone. Like Adam and Eve, we can all find ourselves exiled from Eden, unable to return or even to remember the idyllic days when we walked so easily with God in the garden of our souls. We may be able to name the event or the person who closed the gate behind us when we were cast out and our relationship with God rudely ended. Or we may have simply wandered away on our own, lost our bearings, and not returned.

In spiritual exile we think of God as back there in the garden. We presume that we left God—or God left us—and that we now wander like Cain, alone and cut off from the Holy One. We assume ourselves to be spiritually displaced, religious refugees without passports back to the garden, with no spiritual homeland.

Even committed believers who are faithful to their religious teachings and practices can suffer spiritual exile. They may never leave the religion of their childhood. Deep within, however, there can be a disconnect. The externals of religion do not find beneath the soil of the soul any spiritual waters to absorb and deliver to the branches of doctrine. There are many testimonies in the writings of religious persons about periods of such spiritual exile, even years of spiritual aridity. The spiritual seeker or even the spiritual guide can begin to doubt the truth and validity of relationship with God. Anyone can feel cut off from the Holy One, at least in terms of any felt relationship.

Sometimes religious exile from an organized faith is the beginning of spiritual exile as well. The fault we may find with our religious congregation or church may be only a surface fracture. Deep beneath in the bedrock of the soul there could be a more substantial rift, as heartfelt questions about the existence of God and personal immortality crash against and get buried by immovable objections of logic and reason, or are pulverized by painful personal experience.

The God of No Place

In the ancient Mideast, the homelands of the Hebrews and their neighbors, respectable divinities would never appear or take up residence in deserts. Few if any of the holy spots identified in ancient Near East religions were in the desert. Temples were the stuff of cities. Shrines were surrounded by gardens, not by desert. The forbidding terrain of desert areas was the territory of marauding demons who wandered about in search of the luckless exile. Gods and goddesses dwelt among the gentry, within the security of the ramparts.

Slowly, as the Hebrews discovered and named their sacred places, something rather new and different began to emerge. Their God Yahweh seemed not to need an honored place amidst the city temples and shrines in order to maintain the divine prerogative. The Hebrews slowly achieved religious distinction by a gradual realization that Yahweh was not tied to the usual sacred places. God's place was among the people of Israel, wherever they might be. God, they slowly came to believe, was wherever they were.

Their religious experience was that Yahweh followed them when they were exiled out of the cities and towns of the Promised Land. Even when they were traveling across the deserts, the less desirable supernatural real estate left over to the demons, Yahweh was with them to protect and shelter them. God shared their displacement.

There are early hints in the Jewish scriptures of God's vagabond nature. For it was not in a great city but in the Sinai Desert that the Hebrews as a people had their first formal introduction to God. This encounter happened through the good offices of Moses, who himself, not so long before, had had his first powerful encounter with God before a bush that burned in the heat of the desert. Later, when the Jews suffered exile through the great eastern desert that led into Babylon, they again encountered God in their rereading and rewriting of the sacred texts that they brought with them. In this second great exile of the nation of Israel, the conviction that God was with them in their banishment from Jerusalem and the Promised Land worked its way onto almost every page of the sacred texts from this period. One hears this theme again and again throughout the later chapters of the prophet Isaiah: "For the Lord will comfort Zion; he will comfort all her waste places, and will make her wilderness like Eden, her desert like the garden of the Lord; joy and gladness will be found in her, thanksgiving and the voice of song" (Isa 51:3).

Displaced believers can share this powerful conviction with the people of Israel. Doubt, disbelief, agnosticism, all forms of religious exile, even spiritual exile, do not mean that one has no access to God, no opportunity for meeting the transcendent. Whatever has happened to lead one into religious exile, whatever has caused spiritual displacement, there always remains the assurance, so powerfully attested to in scripture, that God goes with the displaced believer into that exile. God is displaced too. If this is so, then no displacement, no exile of any kind means the end of relationship with God, even if one does not feel particularly connected to this divine fellow refugee.

This Jewish teaching of God's abiding presence with those in exile carries over into the Christian scriptures. As we have seen, they begin with it. The stories of Jesus' birth in the New Testament are framed by exile. He is born in a stable to traveling parents who have just arrived in "the city of David" (Luke 2:4). Birth in a stable may seem exile enough. The last phase, however, intimates the more profound exile. The title "city of David" belonged properly to Jerusalem, which David had chosen a thousand years earlier to be the center of his kingdom (2 Sam 6:6–9). Bethlehem was indeed David's birthplace (1 Sam 16:1–13), but Jerusalem was his city. When the Gospel writer calls Bethlehem "David's city," there is an ironic twist in the text, hinting at Jesus' exclusion from the center of power and prestige, his displacement to the outskirts, his birth in exile.

Exile also closes the early stories about Jesus' beginnings. Within a year or two of his birth, he and his parents are forced to flee from Herod across the Sinai to exile in Egypt. He whom Christians acclaim as Son of God seems to have inherited his father's penchant for out-of-the-way places, a predilection for the displaced.

When Jesus is about to begin his preaching, he once again goes into the desert, driven out by the Spirit, says the Gospel of Mark (Mark 1:12). During the forty years that the Hebrews spent in the Sinai, they met God and got divinely adopted in that deserted place. Jesus seems also to need his forty days and nights of desert exile to consider his own relationship with God the Father. Jesus joins his Jewish ancestors, and the many displaced believers across the ages, in their desert encounters with the divine.

When he returns early in his ministry to his hometown of Nazareth, Jesus is once again exiled, pushed out this time not by the Spirit but by his neighbors. He is excommunicated, expelled from the community, because of his teaching and his claims (Luke 4:28–30). His conviction cost him personal and social exile. Indeed, from this point on he prefers the company of the other social and religious outcasts of his day, even to the point of regularly dining with tax collectors and sinners (Matt 9:10–11; Luke

15:1, 19:7). Finally, Jesus' life story ends as it began. As his birth, so his death occurs outside the walls of David's city, among outcasts and criminals.

The displaced believer can take some comfort from these various exiles of Jesus. He became the companion to exiles, even to those in spiritual exile. From the cross, that instrument of ultimate exile, his final prayer is one of spiritual exile: "My God, my God, why have you forsaken me?" (Matt 27:46; Mark 15:34; Ps 22:2).

Exile and the Spiritual Life

How might one find this displaced God who shares the exile's plight? Where and how does one look to meet or be met by the Holy One who abides somewhere out in the vastness of our own particular deserts? One way is for the exile to become a pilgrim. When displaced and exiled, a person is already on the move one way or another, by force or by choice. The forced march or the flight for safety can be transformed into a pilgrimage for one's own personal benefit. To do this, to convert exile into pilgrimage, a person needs to find his or her own personal sacred places. To change the misfortune one has suffered into an occasion of hope and an opportunity for new life, one must find and visit those sacred times that nourish and nurture the soul.

Certainly those who suffer exile from their homeland or family because of political, social, or religious causes can find comfort, strength, and hope by becoming pilgrims. When a person is far from home, or removed from family affection, or forced to the social perimeter, the interior life becomes all the more important. The interior life of the soul can be the source of new direction and purpose. When everything outside is confused and contrary, distracting and destructive, sacred time and place can provide the respite and relief one needs to continue on. No matter where exile leaves a person in the outside world, the journey within can lead to

God who dwells there. When we travel as exiles, we ourselves are the vessel, the ark that contains the exiled God.

This is true even when it is a personal religious exile we suffer. If we have left or been forced out of our own religion, it is all the more important to become an intentional pilgrim. When our religious home is no longer hospitable or helpful, we need to search the inner landscape of the soul. Those who are deprived for whatever reason of the sacred places of their religious heritage can locate the inner spring or garden, the internal cave or mountain where they sense or suspect the divine presence to dwell in some special way. There, deep within, the religious exile can discover, celebrate, and explore his or her inner sacred places of encounter with the divine. There, in sacred time and in sacred space, the Holy One, our faithful companion in exile, joins in our religious displacement and shares our journey through the wasteland. Our divine co-traveler can speak to us as we walk along together, gently urging us to gain new perspective from our exile, to consider new paths for travel. Like the Jews in their desert exiles, we can receive new and unique revelations of the holy in our own deserts. Like Jesus, pushed into the desert by the Spirit, our religious exile can become a journey that brings us meaning, purpose, and hope.

What, however, of those whose exile is spiritual, whose alienation is not from a particular religion, but from the very idea or experience of the divine? Is pilgrimage of any value for them? Does sacred time and sacred place offer hope or peace for those in spiritual exile?

When considering such questions, it is crucial to respect a person's spiritual exile. We cannot know what has led an individual into his or her spiritual wasteland. There is no easy, prepackaged, dogmatic answer that can whisk a person out of such a place. Yet there is a suggestion that may be of help to those in spiritual exile, wherever their desert paths may ultimately lead them. There is something that the spiritual life, that regular pilgrimage to personal sacred time and place may offer to enrich the lives of spiritual exiles. It is the invitation to interiority.

The value of spiritual pilgrimage, of making space for one's own sacred times and places, is that it tutors us in interiority. Our personal pilgrimages help us approach questions and concerns about God with a deepened sense of soul, a greater appreciation for the complexities within ourselves. All this may not mean that ultimate questions are quickly resolved or that relationship with God is easily restored. However, for those who wish to continue their journey through the spiritual wasteland, the practice of timely pilgrimage to sacred space builds their strength, deepens their empathy, and broadens their horizons.

The first fruit of pilgrimage is a return to our own self, a reconnecting with our own soul. So often we cannot detect the divine presence in our spiritual exile because we have lost touch with our own sense of self. We cannot hear hints of the holy or track traces of the divine along our paths of exile because our souls have gone deaf and blind. The practice of the spiritual life can help us discover or rediscover our own inner self. Then, as we learn to return to and dwell in the deepest parts of our self, the return to God may become a possibility. As we grow accustomed to our sacred time and place, we may catch fleeing glimpses of God or detect quiet whispers of the eternal word. As we dwell more and more within our own being, we may sense the presence and the power of Divine Being.

CHAPTER 3

Return

S ometimes exile is followed by return. Political fortunes change. Refugees may get the opportunity to return to their homeland. It becomes safe to go back and begin the process of rebuilding a life for oneself and for loved ones. Or, if the exile has been from a relationship, there may be reconciliation. Misunderstandings can be cleared up, misgivings assuaged, and mistakes repaired. Forgiveness can open doors once shut tight and locked against any hope of return to love. If an exile has been caused by serious illness, recovery means an eventual return to society, to work, to family. If the exile has been one brought on by the death of a loved one, the period of mourning usually comes to a point where one must decide whether and how to return to life. Bereaved and bereft, one tentatively reenters the stream of daily life to resume some kind of normalcy.

During these many different types of exile, return may be greatly anticipated and longed for. The refugee may think about nothing else but restoration to the homeland, the spurned lover to the former place of affection. The bereaved, shocked by loss, may fantasize about a return to the way life was before the loved one was lost. However, the difficult discovery for every kind of hopeful returnee is that no matter what type of exile one has suffered, the return is never to the way things were.

Negotiating Return from Exile

If those who have been exiled from their country are eventually able to return home, they are often in for an even more difficult adjustment. While they were away, they changed. Their view of the world, their understanding of self, their ways of relating to others all underwent significant and irrevocable changes. They are different in ways they only begin to discover as they attempt to reenter their home country and original culture. Now they know another way of looking at life, at politics, at religion, at family life and social roles, at themselves. Their political innocence and cultural naivete have been lost. In a sense they can never go home again, because the "they" is so different. Too much has changed, both in the refugee who has suffered so much and in the homeland that has endured occupation or devastation. Reentry can be nothing less than a renegotiation.

There is a similar dynamic in cases of personal exile. When friends or couples break up and go their separate ways, their divergent paths take them to different and disparate experiences that change them. If they should come back together after some time, expecting a return to their relationship as it once was, they will be confused and perhaps disappointed. Longing for the relationship they previously had will not help. They need to come to know each other as they are now and build on that new possibility. Our tendency to retreat to the past, with its models and messages, is very strong. We struggle to be attentive to the radical newness of restored relationships, and responsive to their new challenges.

Exile of any type changes us. When we leave the familiar place we have known, we come to see the world from the perspective of our new place. Even if that new place is one of banishment, it nonetheless provides us with a new outlook on things. We see ourselves, others, and the world from different angles. Our priorities shift and rearrange themselves in ways we could never have imagined. Our sense of who we are, what we are worth, and what our accomplishments might be all change. In a very real sense, every exile is final, because every exile changes us by virtue of the experience of being banished, or of simply being away—someplace else. We cannot return to that previous place as it was, because both we ourselves and that place have changed irrevocably during and because of our displacement.

Return to Religion

Some people who have left the religion of their childhood may eventually choose to return. They often assume, usually at unconscious levels, that they are returning to that faith as they once knew it. This cannot happen. The return to the religion of childhood is somewhat like the return of the refugee to her or his homeland. The task in front of the returnee in both cases is one of rebuilding, of making a new life, or a new life of faith. Both the person returning and the religion itself have changed during the separation, like two spouses who have parted ways and later try to get back together. What was past is only prelude.

This can be difficult and surprising for the person who has made the often difficult decision to return to the faith they once knew. After a struggle of conscience and much soul searching, they walk back into that place of childhood memories expecting that it will actually be some type of return to the past. The whole recommitment may have nostalgic overtones for them. They presume that a return to their religion after years of absence will be a wistful affair, affording the soul all the remembered sentiments of childhood.

The reality, of course, is more like the experience of the exile or the émigré who has struggled in the country abroad and who then returns home to face yet another and even more confusing adjustment. There may be some measure of sentimentality, but sooner or later the returning believer is confronted with the challenges and demands of mature faith. Like the spouses who must learn to love beyond romance and into fidelity, the returning adult must negotiate a new relationship with the religion of childhood. It may take time for the person to realize how much they have changed, or how the religion itself has changed. While there may be some comfort and strength in the return to faith, one must eventually assume a much more active position with regard to belief and practice.

There are many kinds of changes awaiting the one who returns to faith. One will notice that friends or family members who have stayed with the religion now relate to it in very different ways. One expects that parents believe and practice their faith just as they did years ago, when the family worshiped together. Those same parents may now be engaged by very different aspects of their faith. What mattered so very much to them in the past has been replaced by new and different concerns. Their aging has itself involved a shifting of priorities in matters of belief. Their prayer and worship may be quite different. Siblings whom one remembers as relating to their faith with devotion or with resentment may have taken different postures. Clergy, the issues they emphasize, official positions taken by the church or congregation, the order of worship: so many aspects of the religion one once knew can be significantly different. Even if the changes, considered one by one, are not so dramatic, when they are all taken together the experience of return can be surprising and even shocking for the person looking for the comforting and secure past associated with religion.

This discomfort can exist even when the person returning to religion has chosen a denomination or a faith different from the one in which they were raised. Joining a new religion involves expectations that things in this newfound faith will certainly be different, and that of course is true. Yet, underneath the allowances for difference, many converts still nurture unspoken hopes that this new faith will satisfy the childhood longing for acceptance and secure love that one's original religion never satisfied. Even conversion to a freely chosen faith in adulthood can still involve regression to early needs. A newly chosen religion may offer comfort, but it will also present challenges and creative confrontations.

Return to Spirituality

As we have seen, spirituality is a person's relationship with God, the Holy One; and the spiritual life is our awareness of, reflection on, and attentiveness to that relationship and its effects on daily life. What might it mean, then, to speak about a return to spirituality? The latter is different from a return to religion. While they are not contradictory, and may even be simultaneous and mutually enriching, the return to religion involves more of a public act and statement. A return to spirituality, on the other hand, is intensely personal. It involves a return to one's more authentic self, to one's interior life, to the pilgrimage within. Like the return to a religious community or church, a return to spirituality can also be difficult and confusing because of the changes in oneself during spiritual exile.

The great model of return from religious and spiritual exile in the Christian writings of the New Testament is the Prodigal Son. This moving parable told by Jesus in the Gospel of Luke (chap. 15), is about a father who has two sons. The younger son requests all of his inheritance, which in that culture was tantamount to disowning his father. He then leaves home for a self-imposed exile in "a distant country," according to the story. There he squanders his inheritance on loose living until he is impoverished. Like a refugee he hires himself out as a laborer, doing tasks that no citizen of this far-off land would do, specifically, feeding and caring for pigs. Pigs were an unclean animal according to the Law of Moses, so Jesus' listeners would understand that this careless lad had not only disowned his father and family, but his whole spiritual tradition as well. His behavior as well as the work he ended up doing confirm the extent of his exile from family and faith.

This son eventually "came to himself" and decided to return home to his father. As he makes the pilgrimage back home, he rehearses in his mind what he will say to his father. His expectations are quite definite and quite low. He will ask to be hired as a laborer on his father's estate and nothing more, hoping he will be lucky enough to get that much. When he is still far off in the distance, his father sees him and rushes out to meet him and embrace him. The grateful father, prodigious in love and forgiveness, orders an immediate feast to celebrate the return of his reckless child.

In this marvelous story we find so many of the elements of both religious and spiritual exile as well as return. The son wanders away from the faith of his family and youth, and repudiates it by his behavior. Then he decides to return, a decision that must have been very difficult and humiliating for him to carry out. In the story the motivation for his decision to return seems at first glance to be complete self-interest. His escapade has left him homeless and penniless, and his father's house holds the solution to his dilemma. One can, however, look deeper into the mind and motivation of the son. During his exile he has come to see everything differently, from the perspective that the "distant country" provided him. He sees his home, his family, his relationships, his faith, even his God from new and revelatory angles. He is a changed man and seeks to test these changes back home.

He does not seem to consider the possibility that during his absence his father has also changed. As he approaches home he braces himself for an encounter that will be difficult. The son thinks his father will react in a certain way, perhaps as he always had in the past. The son seems to take for granted that nothing has changed at home, and that under the rules of the house and of the Jewish faith he will fit back into the household where he now belongs—as a hired hand.

The father, of course, overturns all these reasonable expectations. The son had not counted on the possibility of his father behaving any differently than in the past. The son presumes that since he has broken the Law of Moses in so many ways, his family religion will dictate how he is to be treated. In short, he makes his return with the usual presuppositions that all of us make in similar situations, returning from our different types of exile. He finds that his father, perhaps more narrow and legalistic in the past, has also been changed by the pain of separation and loss. The father has been in his own exile, brought on by the abandonment he felt when the son left. He is different, perhaps radically different, now. His response to the returning son begins a whole new episode in their relationship and in the life and history of their family.

We can easily imagine that the young man, before he so deliberately and dramatically left home, had not thought much about his relationships with his father and other members of the family. He probably saw them only in light of his own needs and wants, and evaluated them insofar as they accommodated him. Upon his return, however, the parable invites us to consider that he will be much more attentive to those relationships and much more intentional about how he engages his family. Certainly, the unexpected reaction of his father upon his return startled the young man into a new openness in their relationship. This is not the father he left, at least from his perspective. One of the things he learns during his return home is that he needs to appreciate how others can change and grow, even as he is realizing how he has changed and grown during the time of his exile. The son will be more attentive to the nature of his relationship with his father, much more intentional about how his behavior will impact that relationship.

The son's situation upon his return is not so different from that of people who have had an experience of exile from personal relationships and who then return. Spouses or friends who have separated, physically or psychologically, and who return to each other do so with certain expectations and assumptions. The reality of the return usually challenges them to rethink those assumptions, to open up their expectations. The other person, like oneself, has been changed by the separation and is different in ways that are both obvious and subtle. It is a new beginning to a substantially new relationship, not just a return to the past.

The return to the spiritual life also requires attentiveness to newness and a readiness to deal with it. We cannot presume that our relationship with God is going to be the same. During the time away, the time of inattentiveness to our relationship with the transcendent, we change. We might even expect that God, or at least our image and understanding of God, has also changed. The return to the spiritual life is not a going back to restore a past relationship. It is a recommitment to a new kind of relationship, to ever new ways of valuing that relationship and ever-changing ways of being intentional about it.

While the return to spirituality can be enriching and invigorating, it can also be disconcerting, because it is not a simple return to former ways of being spiritual. The time of being away, of spiritual exile, has made a difference. It is not a difference that condemns. It is a difference that redeems, that buys back the lost time with the stock of change and new possibilities. But it is a difference, and we must expect and account for it.

Return to God

It may be presumptuous, even misleading, to suggest that God changes. While we, like the prodigal son, are off engaging in other affairs, might God's daily business and worries work changes in the divine personality? Can we imagine that God, like the father in the parable, grows more understanding and merciful? It is perhaps more helpful and to the point to suggest that what changes is our image of God. This is an important distinction that often gets overlooked. There is a difference, an infinitely significant difference, between God as God is and God as we image God. It is not difficult to see this. Presumably, the image of God we have now is different in many ways from the image of God we had five years ago, or ten or twenty years ago. Our image of God grows, changes, and develops in light of our life experience, of our understanding of religious teachings, and of our own spiritual life. It is safe for each of us to count on the probability that the image of God we will have five or ten years hence will again be different from that of the present.

So when we return to a religion, or when we return to the spiritual life, we usually carry in our psychological pockets a different image of the Holy One to whom we are returning. Sometimes we can be quite aware of that. In fact, we may be making the return precisely because our image of God has changed and grown. We may have grown up with the image of a fierce, judgmental, and angry God that has been replaced with a God of mercy and love. We may have once cherished images of God as a benevolent, bearded patriarch, and now are less caught by such anthropomorphic images and more attuned to their metaphysical meanings. We may have traded a tribal God, who loves our kind of people and not the rest, for a more universal God who loves all indiscriminately, with the passionate and prodigious forgiveness of the father in Jesus' parable.

No one person's image of God, even the sum total of all their images of God across a lifetime, can be claimed to represent the totality of the divine. No one image of God from a particular religion, nor the total of the many images of God offered throughout the history of a religion, can be taken to be a full revelation of the totality of the holy. Even Christians, who find in Jesus the ultimate and fullest revelation of the Father, need to remember Jesus' statement: "Where I am going, you cannot come" (John 13:33). Only Jesus' own return to the Father at the end of his life brought about the final and complete divine revelation through Jesus' humanity. Christians celebrate that only through sacrament and symbol, not in any complete, final, and full image.

The return to God, then, is never complete. We are all like the prodigal while he is still on the road to home but not yet there. We can only catch glimpses of God, who is waiting out on the perimeter of the divine estate, scanning the horizon for us as we make our way back. We are not close enough to see the divine face, to catch the details of posture and pose. Each of us will see different things at this distance, which we interpret differently at different times.

Our return requires a constant willingness to give up, to surrender when the appropriate time comes, the particular image or idea of God we might be hiding under our traveling clothes. In a sense the return to God is fraught with a continuing exile, or at least a continuing loss. We must be willing to let go of the presuppositions, the presumptions, the assumptions and answers about God that we have counted on. We need to leave them behind, to discard them along the way. And that is difficult. Difficult because these religious ideas and divine images we cherish give us comfort, give us connection to the past, to our past. So we leave them most unwillingly along the pilgrim road as we travel back, like treasured possessions from a lost home or loved one.

The Many Ways of Return

There is no one right way to make a return to religion, to the spiritual life, to God. There are as many ways as there are believers in exile. Even in the Bible there are a great variety of returns from exile. The story of the prodigal son presents one model for understanding the many dynamics involved in returning to religion or to spirituality. There are other stories about and models of return that express the great diversity of issues and feelings, hopes and concerns of the returning religious or spiritual exile.

The Exodus of the Hebrews from Egypt and their slow journey through the Sinai Desert to the Promised Land is perhaps the greatest of all homecoming stories in the Bible. This was a long and difficult return, full of uncertainty, questioning, contention, and confusion. Moses himself, the leader of the return, was a victim of the journey. The stress of leading a rebellious crowd of returnees led to his own doubting of God and of God's power to save them. Moses does not complete the return. He does not enter the Promised Land. This return of the Hebrews takes forty years, a whole generation. It encompasses a complete life cycle of events, of births and deaths, hopes and disappointments before the home-coming to the sacred places of their ancestors is complete. It was a slow and gradual process of infiltration and assimilation into the land that had been settled by other tribes in the long absence of the descendants of Joseph and his brothers.

For some of us, the return to faith, to a spiritual life and relation-ship with God will be long and arduous, like the return of the Hebrews from Egypt to the Promised Land. We will lose faith and give into our doubts, as Moses did. We will grow quarrelsome and restless, challenging authority and questioning leadership. Like the Hebrews we will break the commandments, and like Moses we will lose patience and perspective. We will complain even when gifted with the many miracles of manna in our personal deserts. Yet throughout it all, God will be with us, as surely as Yahweh God traveled through the Sinai with the Hebrews.

Another great return in the scriptures is that of the Jews from their later exile in Babylon. When Babylon was itself in turn con-quered by Cyrus of Persia, the captive Jews were allowed to return to Jerusalem. So they set out once again, across another desert, trav-eling back to the Promised Land, this time from the East. This return is very different in character from the Exodus return seven hundred years before; this time the exiles return with speed and clear intention. They head, almost unimpeded, toward Jerusalem, and once arrived they set about the immediate task of rebuilding the city and the temple. This expeditious return is accompanied by the consoling words of the prophet that are recorded in the later chapters of the book of Isaiah: "For you shall go out in joy, and be led back in peace; the mountains and the hills before you shall burst into song, and all the trees of the field shall clap their hands"

(Isa 55:12). God's intent is clear. It is to restore Israel and to call the people back to true and committed worship.

Sometimes the return from religious or spiritual exile is just as clear, just as convincing and compelling as that of those Jewish exiles from Babylon. We read in the books of Ezra and Nehemiah how the exiles went about the reconstruction of their religion and the repair and renovation of the Jerusalem temple. Some people who return to their religious or spiritual life do so by intentional study, by the reconsideration and reconstruction of ideas. They find particular spiritual writings and religious teachings to be helpful and encouraging. They return to their houses of worship, or build new ones, with the pride and assurance the Jews had upon their return from Babylon.

In the Christian New Testament there is another story of return. It is that of the magi and their fabled journey, guided by the star to Bethlehem. After their visit with the child Jesus, they begin their return home. They are warned in a dream, however, not to return home by the same and usual route because of the dangerous political situation and King Herod's malicious intentions. This biblical story suggests another kind of spiritual return. There are believers whose return to religion or to spirituality is guided by inner revelations and intuitions. They are led by the light of an inner star, prompted and guided by the Divine One who speaks in their heart. A long way off from the security and safety of their original religious homes and traditions, they follow a different route. Like the magi who had the wisdom to listen to and heed their inner moments of grace and guidance, they find the holy speaks to them in the hidden depths of their humanity. Such attention to the interior life will itself guide them along safer routes as they travel the pilgrim path.

In the early part of Matthew's Gospel, as we have seen, we read the story of yet another exile and return. It is the exile of the child Jesus, with his mother Mary and Joseph into Egypt. As the magi head home toward the East, Joseph is warned to take his family west toward the land of Egypt, where their Hebrew ancestors had once been exiled for centuries. King Herod was seeking to find and kill the child Jesus because he perceived a political threat. So this new Joseph, with his wife and Jesus, retraces the ancient exile of his ancestor, Joseph son of Jacob, across the Sinai into the land of Egypt. The Joseph of ages past was sold by his own brothers as a slave and taken to Egypt. This Joseph flees to protect Jesus, Mary, and himself from the butchery of the Roman puppet King Herod. Both Josephs reflect and foreshadow the multitude of exiles who are banished by betrayal and avarice, by power and politics.

This is an exile of safety. There are those who need to leave the homeland of religion, the shelter of spirituality, because of the threat of danger and betrayal. Some people go into religious and spiritual exile because religion and spirituality are no longer safe for them. It may be that their particular religion is practiced by unhealthy people in destructive ways. Their religious or spiritual well-being is actually threatened by the group to which they belong. It may even be that the spiritual, good in itself, has stifled the growth of their character and the flowering of their personality because of the way they were taught to practice it. Leaving their religion, even their life of prayer, for a foreign land may be their only recourse, their only way of survival, at least for a time.

For these exiles it is of immense importance to listen to the promptings of their souls, the movements of the Spirit within them. Like the magi, warned about which road to take and which to avoid, like Joseph warned in a dream when to leave for Egypt and when to return, such persons are guided and cared for by the Divine One in ways that may elude the comprehension and understanding of others. They will find their way if they learn to listen, to be attentive to the inner life. They will grow "in wisdom and in years, and in divine and human favor," as Luke's Gospel says of Jesus (Luke 2:52).

One final example of return mentioned in the Christian Gospels is that of the disciples back to Galilee. This particular tradition about Jesus' death and resurrection tells of his bewildered disciples being visited by an angel (Matt 28:10,16; John 21). The angel advises them to leave Jerusalem and go back home to Galilee, where they will meet Jesus again, and with his help gradually understand all that has happened.

The disciples had originally left Galilee to follow Jesus. Each left the land of his childhood, the territory of his family's faith and religion. There are believers, who like the disciples of Jesus, leave the territory of their childhood faith and religion. Like the disciples, in order to gain more understanding and be true to themselves, they eventually need to return to the place they left. It is in the return to the religion of their youth, to the familiar sounds and sights, spaces venerated and times celebrated, that they come to fuller understanding of life and of faith. Their return to spirituality involves a return to the richness of their religious tradition and all that it had always offered them, but which they have not been able to appreciate until they had left and come back.

For these people the return will not be a simple going back, but a going back widened, deepened, broadened, and transformed. They will return with a greater capacity to receive what their religion, with its teachings about spirituality, has to offer them. Their return will be, as it was for the disciples when they finally did encounter Jesus back in Galilee, a meeting on a mountaintop. Their return will provide them new perspectives on life and faith. They will see things from their newly rediscovered home that they had never noticed before. Their horizons will be immense and embracing.

The God of Return

When we set about a personal pilgrimage, when we choose to discern and then to visit our own sacred time and place, we are beginning our return. It may be a return to our former religious family, or to a new one. It may be a return to an intentional spiritual life that will enrich us in immeasurable ways within our soul. No one person's return will be quite the same as that of another. We will experience some of the varieties of returns written about in the Bible or even combinations of all of them.

The most important thing to remember is that while we might think of God as waiting there in the distance to receive us upon the final steps of our return to a religious or spiritual life, it is at least as important to see God as returning with us. Just as God is a God of exile, sharing the banishment of the displaced believer, God is also a God of the return, sharing our ways and roads back. God met the Hebrews in the Sinai and traveled with them on their long journey back to the Promised Land. God was exiled with the Jews into Babylon, and returned back with them to Jerusalem. The Holy One guided the magi by the star to Bethlehem; the Holy One was also the inner star that steered them back east safely. The Spirit spoke to Joseph in a dream and remained with him along that well-worn route to and from Egypt. The angel of God prompted the disciples to make the return journey back to Galilee.

Neither in our going away, nor throughout our exile, nor during our return is the holy ever absent. No matter what our location and situation, no matter how prodigal we have become in our life, God is to be found in the midst of it. Spirituality is simply the discovery of that enduring, loving, divine presence. The spiritual life is an intentional accommodation of our daily affairs and concerns to the constant surprise of the Holy One's place at our side and in our heart.

PART TWO

Diligence:
Becoming a Spiritual Pilgrim

*What am I loving
when I love my God?*
Augustine, *Confessions* X, 6, 8

When organized religion is at its best, it not only helps us in our relationship with God, it also addresses three other essential relationships in life. These three are our relationships with our self, with other persons, and with the world we share. Unfortunately, when religion fails us, it is very often a failure in one or more of these three relationships. Religion can hamper or impede how we feel about and understand ourselves. It can confuse or misguide us as we strive to navigate our way through relationships. It can also discourage us from creative engagement with the world and its needs by directing our attention solely to the afterlife.

Religious exile often begins when religion has somehow caused harm in one of these three areas of human engagement with self, others, and the world. A believer may hear Jesus' commandment to "love your neighbor as you love yourself" and feel a big vacuum inside. Instead of love of self, religion may have stressed only self-denial, or even self-hate. Or religion may have emphasized universal love and forgiveness, without addressing the peculiarities and paradoxes that plague every individual and specific relationship. Or religion may have left the devout believer disengaged from the wider human struggle and disenfranchised in the world community. Confusion, frustration, or discouragement in these relationships can mean the beginning of religious displacement.

If religion has caused some kind of disorder in loving, be it in love of self, others, or the world, and has led a believer into exile, personal sacred space and time become very important. They provide the opportunity to reflect on the state of our affections and affiliations. If, in our exile, we set aside space for interior reflection, our understanding of love gets refined and reshaped by the silence.

Our divine fellow refugee can begin to tutor us in intimacy. As we visit our sacred times and places there can be a maturing of affection, a healing of intimacy, a growth in our discernment and discrimination about love. In exile, love can be rediscovered or retrieved as diligence.

Diligence is not just a synonym for *love,* not just a variation of *affection*. It expresses a deeper understanding of the nature and dynamic of love. At first, *diligence* can seem a stern word. We speak of parents striving to be diligent about duties at home or work. Children are schooled to be diligent in their studies. A manager should exercise due diligence in the awarding of contracts; the broker in the making of investment choices. *Diligence* can mean "vigilance, persistence, stick-to-itiveness." There is another meaning of the word, however. It is an older, warmer, more engaging meaning, closer to the word's Latin root *diligere*— "to love or to care for." *Diligence* means "to approach the person or task at hand with loving care." It describes an approach not only of love, but of love and care, or of love that cares.

One of the gifts of grace that can come to the person in exile is this appreciation of diligence. It is diligence, in its threefold fullness of loving care for one's self, for others, and for the world, that can change the religious exile into a spiritual pilgrim.

CHAPTER 4

Loving Care for One's Self

The first of the three kinds of diligence is self-diligence, loving care for one's self. Unfortunately, religion can throw up roadblocks around self-diligence, preventing people access to it. Christianity, for example, has often preached self-sacrifice and self-denial. Some people raised in various Christian denominations may never have been encouraged to practice a loving care for themselves. In fact, they may have been exhorted to do the opposite: to despise their very self. There have been whole religious and spiritual movements in Christianity that have equated holiness with the renunciation of one's self.

In the Jewish tradition there are strands of self-deprecation. The Wisdom books of the Hebrew scriptures speak often about deference to others and counsel a kind of self-abasement before others. Before the divine majesty, each of us is, according to Wisdom literature, small and ignorant. This has sometimes been interpreted in ways that lead to self-abasement and persistent guilt.

In Hinduism the self is understood to be an illusion, a passing phenomenon, like a momentary ripple that forms and vanishes on the surface of the great ocean of being. Hardly something to take the time to be diligent about. In the strict practice of

Buddhism, the adherent is schooled in behavior and practice designed to teach transcendence of the self. This goal is sometimes even expressed as the annihilation of the self, so that one can be freed from its demands and limitations. The religions of the world seem to cast a great variety of aspersions upon the self; they can be understood, or misunderstood, to hold self suspended in suspicion.

There is certainly enough selfishness and self-indulgence in the world to see why religions offer their counsel on various types of self-denial and self-discipline. We do need to learn to control our needs and rein in our desires. However, such religious rhetoric about the perils of the self has left many devout souls impotent regarding self-diligence. They take spiritual injunctions to deny self seriously. They live disciplined lives and strive to put the needs of others and the mission of their church or congregation before their own needs or desires. There can be heroism here and holiness as well. There can also be frustration, resentment, and despair.

The problem with self-denial and self-sacrifice is that often a believer has never taken the time or found the encouragement to get to know and appreciate the very self they want to surrender back to God. You cannot give a gift that you do not have. Many will join a religious rush to self-sacrifice before they really have a healthy, unblemished self to bring to the altar. It is one thing to devote one's self, heart and soul, to God in such a way that one is aware of the dimensions and mature about the implications of such a heroic act. It is quite another to surrender to God a self that is only dimly aware of what is going on and hardly able to imagine the worth of what was first received from God and what now one is so eager to return. Rather than care for and heal a troubled self, a believer may rush to stuff it in a box and send it off to God.

An analogous situation can be found in marriage. If two people each have a good sense of themselves, if they have grown in self-knowledge and self-respect, then their mutual donation of love and exchange of vows is a powerful witness to love and commitment. If, on the other hand, a person is alienated from self, does not have much insight into self, and has not practiced a loving care for self, the commitment she or he strives to make to the other is hampered and impeded. In cases where both people entering a marriage have little self-knowledge and practice little self-diligence, the relationship will be troubled. We do not have to be perfect to give our selves to God. Yet if we are more aware of and diligent about the gift of self that God has given us, then our relationship with the God to whom we want to give our self will be deeper, richer, and fuller.

There is another frequent problem with a spirituality that puts self-denial and self-sacrifice front and center. Its devotees often end up spending an inordinate amount of time concentrating on the rebellious self that they are trying to corral and control. Self-denial can lead to an obsessive preoccupation with the self. Self-sacrifice can encourage a kind of narcissistic focus on one's religious persona at the expense of others and of God, who purportedly should be the beneficiaries of one's religious sentiment. When our spiritual practices take precedence over the needs of those who depend on us, we may be putting self ahead of others even as we strive to become selfless. Our constant attention to self-denial insulates us from our responsibilities to love others.

The New Testament tells us that Jesus called his followers to a life of self-denial and sacrifice. However, it also quotes him as preaching that the second commandment—to love one's neighbor as one's *self*—is like the first commandment that concerns our love of God (Matt 22:37–40). So many of us struggle with loving God and our neighbor because we have not quite figured out how to love our self. So many devoted religious people rush to love others and God without first taking stock of themselves, without first caring for the gift from God that makes love of others possible in the first place—the gift of one's self.

Original Self-Exile

It is important, even crucial, that religious teaching and spirituality include a healthy, balanced understanding of and appreciation for one's self. There are enough forces in life that militate against loving care for one's self. A particular and pervasive distress to self-diligence is a radical, chronic condition that afflicts the self from the earliest years of one's life. We can call it "original self-exile": original, because it has its roots in the very beginnings of a person's life, in infancy and childhood; self-exile, because it leaves a person alienated from his or her sense of self and almost incapable of practicing any measure of self-diligence.

Learning to care lovingly for oneself begins at birth. During the early months and years of life, a child constantly presents a multitude of needs to its parents and other caregivers. On a physical level alone, a child needs to be fed and bathed, changed and clothed, held and protected. On an interpersonal level, infants respond to the interest and attention, the soothing voice and smiling face we present them. Children are stimulated and energized by the human warmth and interaction that color their field of vision and tickle their alert ears. They return our comforting touch and loving embrace with hands that reach out and eyes that take us in.

When children enter a world like this, a world that responds to their needs, that recognizes their wants and affirms their spontaneity, then they learn about love. When children are born into a nurturing, responsive environment, they naturally and gradually come to know and value themselves. All children are eager students of self-diligence, each in his or her own way. When we love them in the many different ways that meet their needs, they learn how to love themselves. Little by little, in almost unnoticed and imperceptible increments, a child begins to relate to all the various dimensions of self, because we have shown them how by our loving them. This gradual internalization of self-diligence is part of the long and promising journey of infancy, childhood, and adolescence.

Unfortunately, some children get left along the psychological roadside early in this journey. Perhaps a parent was overwhelmed by her or his own needs. Financial problems, or work-related stress, or illness, or abuse from a spouse can each compromise or frustrate our attempts to be good and loving parents. Maybe the child was unwanted in the first place, or separated early from anyone who could have cared. In such situations where there is chronic, critical, and continuous absence of loving care for a child, alienation from self is born. When we repeatedly fail to give children their early lessons in loving, or when that early loving is stingy, conditional, and sporadic, they miss their primary schooling in self-diligence. Their capacity for self-love atrophies like a weak, stringy muscle that fails to develop with the rest of their body and soul. Self-diligence is paralyzed, palsied. Victims never learn how to love and care for themselves adequately. Expressed more radically, they have no felt experience of a self. It is missing, because it was never loved into being.

People who are so unfortunate as to be born into such circumstances often grow into adolescence and adulthood still seeking the basic love and care they missed out on in their early lives. They think that they must constantly work at impressing others, so that others will notice them and perhaps respond to them with interest, concern, and admiration. They learn techniques of getting attention and being noticed. They develop ways of pleasing others and anticipating the wants and desires of others, so that others will like them, maybe even love them. They seem to be on a continuous and misguided quest for the grail of the missing self, asking here and searching there for anyone who might know about it. Such a life becomes one of constant vigilance. Those who have little or no sense of self, who seriously doubt their own worth, must constantly scan the social environment, ceaselessly survey their surroundings, and persistently probe people to assess and anticipate what others might want.

Sometimes, these unfortunate persons are clever and correct in reading and pleasing others, but just as often they misread the situation. Thinking that we will be impressed by their achievements or accomplishments, they create an imposing persona. Such people extol their own deeds and endeavors to win our approval. They tell us about their high-paying jobs and important positions. They intimate or even brag about their sexual prowess and conquests. They allude to their religious superiority or moral integrity, perhaps even to their history of impressive self-sacrifice. They may seek our attention and concern by feigning disease or distress. In fact, they end up by overwhelming and alienating us. Without meaning it, they leave us doubting their worth and suspecting their goodness. Just like them, we wonder who and where the real self is. We, like them, cannot love that self because it is so hidden and elusive, so spectral and fleeting.

At other times a person who is seeking love and acceptance will read our minds and hearts rather well. They will be exceptionally adept at saying what makes us feel good about ourselves. They will have an uncanny knack of sharing our tastes or appreciating our efforts. But there will be a price. If we do not respond to their unspoken requests for love and acceptance, we will eventually receive their anger. When their subtext of approval goes unrecognized and their attention unrequited, the whole relationship begins to turn sour, often in confusing and contradictory ways. When we fail to conjure up for them the self they are missing, they may banish us along with their self to their own personal netherworld.

As adults such people are still seeking the basic love and care that was missed in infancy and childhood. Being in relationship with them is like caring for a demanding child. No matter how much loving we give, no matter how much attention and approval we extend, it is never enough. There is a psychological black hole in the soul of such persons. It threatens to swallow up anything and anyone in its orbit.

This original wound of profound self-exile can lead to so many other kinds of exile and human suffering, infecting all of a person's relationships. It is often hidden beneath excessive self-indulgence and selfishness. It leaves a person incapable of loving care for either themselves or others. It can even contaminate a believer's relationship with God. Spiritual exile, the experience of alienation from God, can sometimes be the result of alienation from self. If God dwells within us, but we cannot venture there, then self-exile can indeed be the cause of spiritual exile.

While we might not all have suffered such radical failures in parenting that we are left almost bereft of self, we all know to some extent what *self-exile* means. We all know what it means to lose our sense of self, at least for a time. We can all empathize with those who suffer the more profound kind of self-exile from childhood. Religion can be a force for good when it provides support and strength for parents and families, translating the love of God into a loving home where children are welcome, lovingly cared for, and tutored in the self-diligence that will become the foundation for a diligent life.

Self-Compromise

Problems in self-diligence are due not only to failures in parenting or to misguided religion. We also can do damage ourselves by self-compromise. We can slowly get into a pattern of decisions or choices wherein we forget about or lose our sense of self as we struggle to negotiate the many difficulties and dilemmas of daily life. We can make choices that undercut our self-worth or confuse our image of who we are. We can hide behind our public persona. We can ignore the deeper meanings of our experience, or fail to chart directions for our future in light of our authentic needs and chosen values. We make such self-compromises amidst the deeds and decisions, the struggles and confusions that comprise the daily patterns of our relationships and of our work.

There are certain relationships that slowly erode our sense of self. These relationships surreptitiously sap us of vitality and conviction. In this type of romance or friendship or work relation-ship, we gradually lose our sense of self, often before we realize it is happening. The relationship may be obviously toxic. The way the other treats us, the unrealistic demands she or he puts on us can, lit-tle by little, poison our sense of self. We grow less and less diligent about our self. We get moody or defensive. We forget which are the legitimate needs of the other, and we overlook the authentic needs of our self. We can end up, eventually, having forgotten completely who we are or were. We have compromised our self in trying to negotiate this kind of relationship.

We can also compromise our self at work. If we are among the fortunate, we take pleasure and derive satisfaction from our work. Our job may even be more than a means to income; it may be a vocation, a calling, a way of contributing to society. There are even those whose occupation, because it is so rooted in their souls, becomes part of who they are, part of their very self. In this situation there is a wise investment of the self in one's work, a way of practicing self-diligence in the tasks and service of everyday life.

There is such a thing, however, as over-investing one's self in work. Especially in America, examples abound of people whose excessively long workdays and workweeks keep them from engaging in other parts of their lives. Home, family, leisure, and hobbies are slowly pushed to the periphery, eventually edged out of sight and out of mind. Time with friends, enjoyment of art and culture, and the quiet downtime we all need to replenish and recreate our selves get lost and forgotten about. Work can become a deal with the devil where not only one's soul, but all of one's self has been contracted, collected, and compromised. The company owns your self, and you don't get visiting privileges. Work, like unhealthy, compromising relationships, can leave the self comatose.

What Is the Self?

What does it mean, then, to care lovingly for oneself? What is this self that we need to be diligent about, yet are so often unaware of or unresponsive to? Self is a subtle and elusive reality, difficult to define or describe. Our eyes can catch the light of a faint star or distant galaxy in the night sky better when we do not fix our gaze directly. Similarly, we observe the self more effectively when we let our mind's eye dance about its perimeter, knowing that its core is always a somewhat distant mystery. We can make various observations about the self, allowing that what we describe may not capture its full meaning.

We can say, for example, that the self includes but is not limited to self-image, that picture or representation that we have in our minds about who we are and how we appear to others. The self also involves but is not defined by our persona, that is, those parts of ourselves that we choose to present to others and allow them to see. It contains but is more than our shadow, those parts of personality and behavior that are hidden and obscured from our own awareness. Self embraces our self-worth but is not constrained by it or by the lack of it. Image, persona, awareness, and worth are all issues that involve self, but no one of them, nor all of them together, constitute the self.

Self also involves an awareness of the wellsprings of our particularity and individuality as persons. Each of us has certain likes and dislikes, particular needs and desires. We are each more or less comfortable with certain kinds of people, and more or less committed to this or that cause or value. Self includes all of these attitudes and dreams, hopes and fears that are particular to a person. Self involves our attention and responsiveness to such things, to their origins within us, and to the distinctiveness they give each of us as individuals. Yet, self is not to be identified with our particularity.

Self also embraces our history, our family background, our choices, and the paths we have traveled in life. In this sense, self is constantly in flux and change. Each choice we make or experience we have, each reflection on experience, becomes a part of our sense of self. Our self is the text of our life story written in our hearts, waiting to be read, interpreted, and continued. Self includes and involves, embraces and contains all these various parts of our personal experience and our history.

Yet, there is still another dimension of the self. Deep within each of us there is a center that ever eludes our focus, which cannot be captured in any abstract snapshot. Like the star that seems to disappear when we look straight at it, the center of the self recedes into the mystery of the infinite. This part of us, that which touches the transcendent, is often called the soul. Because of the soul, we cannot finally achieve a definition of self, we cannot pretend to capture its full meaning and expanse in words. So what we have here is really just a description of the various aspects of self, some broad brushstrokes that help to outline or frame our discussion of self-diligence. To push for more definition would leave less room for the mystery that is at the very heart and source of who we are.

Out of the conviction of religious faith, one can understand the mystery of self ultimately in light of our relationship with the Creator. A human being has and is a self because she or he comes from the mystery of God and stands always in relationship to that divine mystery. The self is ultimately mysterious because it comes from and seeks to return to God.

Self-diligence is the loving care we extend to all these various and complex aspects of our self. The practice of self-diligence attends at different times and according to our changing needs to particular parts of the self. It cultivates care for our personal histories and seeks to discern meaning and direction in the events and experiences of our lives. Ultimately, self-diligence involves a loving care for the soul, a reverence for the mystery at the core of the self.

The Spiritual Life and the Return to Self

The spiritual life is not a panacea. Defects in self-diligence cannot be changed simply by prayer. The wounds of ill-advised self-sacrifice may need many sorts of soothing compounds to be closed and healed. Self-indulgence needs to be challenged and self-compromise confronted. Profound self-exile usually needs professional help and counseling.

A balanced, discerning spiritual life, however, can help us grow in self-diligence. In our appreciation of self, we can be greatly aided by the habit of visiting our sacred time and place, by regular pilgrimages to our personal holy space. Attention to the spiritual life can become an important ally for growth in self-diligence, because sacred time and place provide us with the opportunity to listen to our self and to perceive the truer, deeper nature of our relationships with others.

Much of what we do and of what is done to us throughout everyday life drowns out the voice of the self. What our self tells us about our needs can easily be overpowered by other voices outside of us. A market economy is always telling us what we need. Advertising assaults us from the time the clock radio goes off until we fall asleep during the evening news. Sounds and sights of every conceivable shape and conceit compete for our attention every hour of the day, from the grocery store checkout line to the highway billboards leading home. We are offered endless, contradictory counsel about what we really need, or should believe we need.

Self-indulgence is fed by all this advertising. The self-indulgent person may seem to be very concerned and caring about the needs of the self. Self-indulgence, however, is less a response to the felt needs of our authentic self and more often a dizzy dance we do to the tune piped to us by marketers and hucksters. Self-indulgence meets an agenda set for us by others, and usually for their benefit rather than ours. What fuels such selfish acquisitiveness comes from a culture that seeds and feeds our souls with notions of all those things we need because others already have them, or soon will. Sacred time and place provide some refuge from this frantic fray. The quiet of this time and place is not only an escape from all the distracting noise. It is also an opportunity to listen within, to give space and time to the self and entertain what it has to say to us about what we truly need and desire, rather than what others, society, or the market dictate to us. Quiet becomes a door through which we go to visit our self, to come aside and rest awhile, to dwell in the more authentic parts of our being. The gift of the quiet afforded by sacred time and space provides us the occasion to listen to our self, to the whispers and faint sounds that emerge from the very depths of our being.

In sacred space, while we may be aware of problems and concerns from our daily lives, they do not consume us. As we visit our sacred space more frequently, problems, worries, and concerns recede more readily into the background. This quiet may not be free of uncomfortable feelings or disturbing distractions. In fact, at the beginning of a person's attempt to enter sacred time and space, feelings and issues that have been ignored or repressed may come flooding in. In a society that does not encourage taking quiet time for oneself, it is common that our early attempts to retreat to sacred space get filled with unfinished business from our emotional life. When we first begin to make time for visits to sacred places, we can be overcome with feelings not yet dealt with. Perhaps dealing with such unfinished business might be the first task in a person's spiritual pilgrimage. Or maybe this needs to be dealt with in other, therapeutic contexts. Eventually, as one makes visiting sacred space a habit, emotions and feelings from relationships and work quiet down. One dwells more and more in a sacred silence.

This quiet interiority invites us not only to listen to our own self. After a while our sacred time and place allow us to hear and see the others in our lives in new and revealing ways. The interiority and quiet of sacred time and space can actually open us up to others in ways not possible during the normal give and take of everyday life. Such inner hospitality can help us bring a proper proportion to our relationships. As we have seen, some relationships can cause us to forget or lose our self. Perhaps we have over-invested our self in a friendship or romance. Or maybe we have stayed with someone despite the harm they do to our self or the distraction they cause in our soul. We may have lost all sense of purpose and proportion in certain relationships, compromised and forfeited our self, until we feel helpless to find our way back.

Inner hospitality offers the time and space to discern what it is that we truly want and need in our relationships. At the same time it gives us a chance to bring those others, even the more difficult ones, into our sacred time and place with us. These others share in our inner life through our thoughts and memories of them. This spiritual dwelling together can often help us recover healthier ways of relating to others. When we allow the image or memory of another to inhabit our inner life, the various dynamics of our relationship with them can become clearer.

Inner hospitality helps us consider the reality of who others are to and for our self. We dwell together, corralled by sacred time and space, without the distractions and conventions of everyday life. The possibility of different modes of relationship, of freer and less demanding ways of interacting can also be entertained. When others become part of our spirituality and prayer, the difficult and confusing aspects of our relationships with them can be held up for healing and hope. Sacred space can slowly become an opportunity for relatively nonthreatening encounters with others. One can begin to consider them for who they are, rather than for simply what they can offer or mean to me. We can even find the strength to make the changes in such relationships that self-diligence requires.

The Self and God

As we have seen from the Hebrew scriptures, God goes into exile with those who are banished, for whatever reason. The political exile, the religious refugee, the social outcast all share in the divine presence, all benefit from the divine prerogative to dwell with those who suffer exile.

This same scriptural truth holds for self-exile. Self-compromise may have left us empty and desolate. Immature religious sentiment and ill-advised, ill-timed self-sacrifice may have wasted our good intentions and overspent our good will. Or we may have been wandering the barren, hapless desert of painful exile from the self since our childhood. Whatever our situation, no kind or degree of self-exile is off limits for the holy. No self-alienation is beyond the divine pale.

The Book of Deuteronomy in the Hebrew scriptures presents a powerful, poetic image when it describes God wandering through a desert and discovering an abandoned child. Referring to the people of Israel, the text reads, "He sustained him in a desert land, in a howling wilderness waste; he shielded him, cared for him, guarded him as the apple of his eye" (Deut 32:10). What better image of the lost or exiled self? Even if we have lost our sense of self, God has not lost track of us. God pitches a tent along the bleak and desolate trails of self-exile to wait for the opportunity to shield us, care for us, and guard us.

There are stories in sacred scripture that illustrate God's saving, healing presence for the person who has lost a sense of self. We will consider two of them here. In 1 Kings, we find a story about the prophet Elijah. He is fleeing into the desert to escape the fury of Queen Jezebel, against whose idolatry he has been preaching and stirring up opposition. His sermons as well as his political stance have pushed him into exile, into the desert. Yet it is more than a political exile, more than religious banishment. He seems to have lost himself amidst the controversies and conflicts of the day. "It is enough; now, O Lord, take away my life, for I am no better than my ancestors" (1 Kgs 19:4).

On his flight into exile he comes to Mount Horeb and finds there a hidden cave. His difficult journey of exile has brought him to a sacred place. There, at the mouth of the cave, on the revered mountain of Horeb, Elijah encounters the Holy One. His flight into the desert has become a pilgrimage to a sacred place and a sacred time. As we have seen, in many ancient and contemporary religious traditions, the cave and the mountaintop often appear as sacred places, offering both respite and perspective. These two sacred places are not only goals of the pilgrim's journey; they are also symbols of the inner pilgrimage that the seeker makes to his or her own self. Entry into the sacred cave is a descent into one's own soul. Ascent of the sacred mountain is a retreat to solitary heights where one encounters both God and one's self. The pilgrim's path is a passage to interiority, a Passover to the self and to God who waits there.

At the mouth of his mountain cave, Elijah encounters the Holy One not in the thunder or wind of a desert storm; he senses the presence of God in "a sound of sheer silence," a stirring of God's abiding Spirit (1 Kgs 19:12). The spiritual life is not only a return to God; it is also an invitation to return to our self. Our sacred time and place, our personal pilgrimages provide us the chance to be quiet, so that we might be able to hear the sounds of sheer silence breathed to and in and through our self by God's Spirit. The quiet interiority of sacred time and space help us to listen both to God and to our self, to hear what we truly need and desire. Quiet becomes a path we follow to visit our self, to dwell in the more authentic parts of our being. There, as we begin to listen to the quiet of our deepest self, we can, like Elijah, also hear the voice of God.

The return to self can be difficult and frightening. Those who suffer difficult kinds of self-exile, who have been fleeing like Elijah through a desert of self-alienation, might fear what they will confront in the cave or glimpse from the mountain. What ghosts may lurk within, what echoes of an abandoned self? What distant and forgotten lands can be seen from the heights? For these reasons the practice of spirituality can be very difficult. If we have forgotten or lost our self, then the first challenge of spirituality will be that invitation to go within and slowly get to know or recover our own self. For those who have been missing a self because of their early family experience, interiority presents a special challenge as one comes closer and closer to meeting that authentic self.

The second scriptural story about self-diligence takes place way to the north of Horeb, far from Elijah's desert sojourn. In Samaria there was another holy mountain, Gerizim, sacred to the Samaritan sect who would go there to worship centuries after Elijah's time. In the shadow of this mountain, another encounter between God and self takes place. Jesus had stopped to rest during his journey through Samaria when he met a Samaritan woman at the well in Shechem near Mount Gerizim (John 4). She had come to the well to draw water, little expecting that her daily trek would become a pilgrimage on that particular day. Yet there at the well she meets the one she would come to know as the font of life.

Jesus quickly pulls her into a religious discussion, first about religious and social differences between Jews and Samaritans—two groups that had in essence exiled each other—then about himself, and finally about her self. In fact, Jesus does what we might call in today's terms a "self-inventory," reviewing her marriages, her religious practices, and her past so thoroughly that she testifies to her friends, "He told me everything I have ever done" (John 4:39). Her encounter with Jesus became an encounter with her self. As this woman, following Jesus' prompting, enters more deeply into the mystery of her own self, she also begins to realize the mystery of Jesus' self. Encounter with and acceptance of her self opens the possibility of her encounter with the Holy One before her. Her daily chore of drawing water becomes a sacred moment through which she enters the mystery of her self and the presence of God.

When we go to our sacred places and set aside our sacred times, we bring our self with us. We may feel like Elijah, losing a grip on our self, just wanting it all to end. Or we may be like the Samaritan woman, submerging our true self under all sorts of relationships and distractions. No matter what our sense of self may be, the practice of the spiritual life will sooner rather than later bring us face to face with the deeper parts of who we are. That encounter may bring healing and strength, so that like Elijah we can continue our journey. At other times it will stop us in our tracks and turn us around, as Jesus did to the woman at the well. If we continue our practice of personal pilgrimage, regularly seeking sacred time and place, our spiritual life will bring us ever deeper into the mystery of our self, into the mystery of the soul where God dwells, waiting to love us into self-diligence.

CHAPTER 5

Loving Care for Others

E very exile is a crisis in love. If we are in personal exile, because a relationship has ended and we are left alone, then we may feel that we have failed at loving. We might even wonder if we are at all capable of intimacy. Or, when we suffer social exile, shut out or shunned because of who we are or what we think, we are also thrown into a crisis of love and intimacy. Our very self is denigrated by those who drive us out. How can we then go on loving them, or even loving ourselves, when we have been so devalued? Even those in political exile find that their most reliable relationships are strained and stressed under the burdens and humiliations of banishment. As their exile lengthens, it becomes more and more difficult to sustain love. Intimacy becomes an indulgence too rich and risky for the refugee.

Religious exile can also mean crises in our relationships. When we leave our religion, we often leave friends and family behind as well. Parents or siblings cannot understand our reasons and decisions and may feel betrayed. Or friends who might be indifferent about our religious choices seem distant to us, because they cannot appreciate how difficult those choices have been. Leaving a religion, or being driven out, is also a crisis in intimacy with our own self. If religion has been a part of our lives since childhood, going out the door means abandoning part of our very self, part of who we had been or had once hoped to be. Religious exile involves much more than religious choices or changes. It deeply affects many of our affiliations.

Likewise, spiritual exile also raises questions about intimacy. For many people God is, as Saint Augustine wrote, "closer to me than I am to myself." If our relationship with God is on hold, if we doubt or despair of ever again having God as our all-knowing and all-loving conversation partner, then intimacy is indeed in crisis. Its possibilities become radically different without the divine.

Crises of love and intimacy bedevil exiles of all types. Yet, the very displacement that defines our exile can be an opportunity to reflect on the state of our affections. When we step aside or are pushed aside, we do gain at least the one advantage of perspective. We can see intimacy from a new angle, scrutinize love from a different point of view. However painful the dislocation may be, when love is studied in exile, it can be recognized in new ways. Diligence, as it takes root in the depths of our soul, branches out to care lovingly for others. Loving, thoughtful care for one's self naturally seeks to care lovingly for others. Yet, just as we struggle to practice authentic self-diligence, we also falter and fail in our loving care for others.

For one thing, our relationships can confuse us. We can get tangled in their web, caught by the complexities of our motivations and feelings, snarled by disappointment and rejection, twisted and tousled by the expectations and demands of family, friends, and acquaintances. To distinguish categories or kinds of loving can help us understand our motives, discern our feelings, and discriminate among the values and hopes we bring to relationships. Such distinctions can enrich our diligent love of others. They can also help us to bring those we love into our spiritual lives. The more we understand about those we love and the ways we love them, the more we enrich the inner hospitality of our spiritual lives. Our sacred times and places become not so much an escape from others, but a sanctuary into which we can bring them, and our loving care for them.

Romance and the Spiritual Life

The kind of relationship about which most songs are composed, into which we fall most easily, and from which exile can be so painful is romance. We all know about romance, if not firsthand at least from a distance. One knows not why or how, but another person, perhaps all of a sudden, perhaps slowly and at first imperceptibly, becomes the center of the universe. Wherever he or she is at any given moment becomes the *axis mundi,* the point around which the Earth turns, the Garden of Eden and gate of heaven. All of life gets rearranged. Priorities shift. Schedules are shuffled. Other relationships are altered. New energy surges through one's mind and body. Poetry flows from one's pen, and pain is borne with abandon.

Some interpret the experience of falling in love as nature's way of ensuring the continuation of the species, a genetic characteristic of evolutionary success. Romantic love, in this approach, is no more than a social cover for lust. The point of it all is to copulate and propagate. The deed done, feelings will soon ebb, and one is left alone on the shore watching the storm recede at sea. Sooner or later, one will once again be engulfed in another romantic tempest, as life seeks a way to continue itself. Such a pragmatic take on romance makes it hard to find much meaning in it all. Our bodies and feelings are vessels used by Mother Nature to carry her treasures from one generation to the next.

This utilitarian, evolutionary understanding of romantic love stands in stark contrast to the ideal of romance found in medieval culture and literature. This latter, more idealistic approach makes a clear distinction between romantic love and lust. Lust, the desire to enjoy the body of another, is an appetite. It is indeed our animal nature ensuring its own future as a species. It is powerful, to be reckoned with and tamed by a social order that is just as necessary for our common survival.

Romantic love in the more idealized view, however, is not an appetite; it is a feeling. *Feeling* is a difficult word to define. When we try to craft a definition to explain what feeling is, we often resort to examples or kinds of feeling such as happy, sad, afraid, angry. But all feeling can be explained or described as a way of valuing. Whatever the particular kind of feeling we might have about another person or situation, the nature and strength of that feeling is a measure of the value we place on the individual or event. If we get angry with a person, it is because we value that person, or because what they have done affects someone or something of value to us. If we are happy about something, our joy is a measure of the importance of what has happened in our lives. We do not develop strong feelings toward persons or about situations that do not somehow carry meaning and purpose for us.

Romantic love, while it may involve and incite our lustful appetite, is in and of itself a feeling, a way of valuing. When we are in love with someone, the beloved holds immense value for us. His or her welfare, happiness, health, physical being, the totality of who and what the beloved is, becomes tremendously important for us. Our feelings about our beloved are barometers of the value and priority she or he has for us. The strength, intensity, and passion of our feelings when we are in romantic love are measures of the significance, worth, and meaning that the relationship has in our lives.

As a way of valuing, romance takes us over. Whether we fall for an idealized and unreachable woman or man, or for the boy or girl down the street, romantic love encompasses us with its swirl of feelings and emotions. The beloved assumes immense and overwhelming importance and value for us. The depth of our feelings about the beloved is proportional to the value they hold for us. Yet romance will fade, or at least will lessen in intensity. We may eventually fall in love again, with the same person or with someone else. Romance comes and goes in our lives, like the tides that ebb and flow, which are sometimes at high flood and sometimes withdrawn far from the shore.

Romantic love, however, changes us with its comings and goings. One who has been in love, who has loved immensely and intensely for a time, is a different person for that experience. To fall in love, to hold another person to be so important, of such value and consequence for us, is to be displaced. When we are in love, it is the beloved who displaces us. He or she takes center stage in our attention and affection. We are literally, and willingly, put out. We might say that romantic love involves an experience of ecstasy, of being out of ourselves and absorbed in the other.

Because it involves being so radically displaced from the center of our own attention, and because it entails going out of and beyond ourselves, romance can be thought of as preparation for spiritual experience. The nature of spiritual experience, of relationship with God, also involves a kind of self-displacement. It is like falling in love insofar as our attention and intention, our vision and focus are not on ourselves, but on the Holy One. This is especially true for those who remain committed to the spiritual life, who persist along the pilgrim way year after year. Even as they grow in self-diligence, their value and concern become ever more centered on God. Strong religious experiences may even include ecstasy, an experience of going out of or beyond ourselves and into the holy. Some mystics have described their deeply religious experiences as a "falling in love with God." Even if there is not a strong emotional or affective component to our own spiritual experience, encountering the holy in our sacred space always holds the possibility of being displaced by and through the passionate divine lover who is the center and source of all that is.

Romantic love may be a dimension of our species' way of propagating itself. But it may also be one of God's ways of tutoring us in ecstasy, of luring us out of our selves to encounter another fully and completely. Romantic love then can become a preparation for and even a dimension of displacement by the holy when we enter our sacred spaces.

Friendship

One of the most chilling phrases the thwarted suitor might hear is, "I consider you a friend." Compared to romantic love, friendship seems tame. When one is romantically in love, the beloved is to be completely possessed, without rival. Jealousy stands guard at the palisades, and one wants to be alone with the beloved as much and as often as possible.

We treasure our friends, but we don't bury them with the kind of feverish overprotectiveness reserved for our lovers. Friendship seems more a matter of choice than of fascination and fixation. C. S. Lewis offered one of the best explanations of the origin of friendships. He thought that what binds two people together in friendship is a common difference they share, something that sets them "apart together" from the crowd.

How do we choose certain people from among the many we meet to be our friends? If we follow Lewis's lead, it is because we discover that with this particular person we have something in common, something of importance to us. It may be a casual conversation that reveals how an acquaintance has, like us, come from the same part of the country, or from the same ethnic background, or from the same kind of dysfunctional family. It may be we discover that a person whom we have known for a long time shares our interest in a certain author, in a certain kind of music or art, a particular sport or hobby. Or we may have a particular kind of life experience in common. It could be an illness, a divorce, children the same age, childlessness, bereavement, birth, religion, occupation. Something about the other catches and keeps our interest. When the interest is mutual and reciprocated, friendship can be born.

Though it does not need the passionate pledges of the earnest lover, friendship does require a commitment of time and communication. It calls for continuing interest and reliable response, of being there when needed and of being able to take up the relationship easily and eagerly after months or years of absence.

When we do give friendship the consideration it deserves, it rewards us with companionship and comradeship that is truly irreplaceable. One of the great gifts of diligence is to share friendship with and among a number of common friends. When we discover not just one, but several others who share with us and with each other a common interest, a unique and unifying purpose, our lives are immeasurably enriched.

Spiritual Friendship

It is a powerful and even astonishing experience to discover another person, or if one is fortunate, a group of persons who share an interest in and concern about the spiritual life. In modern Western societies, religion and spirituality are so often considered to be private matters, deeply personal and therefore, many wrongly conclude, desperately solitary and secretive. There are, to be sure, denominations and congregations that encourage public expressions of faith and religious feeling. There are styles of worship and prayer meetings that allow and foster shared expressions of faith and religious sentiments. However, there is not necessarily a movement from the common and shared expression of religious sentiment and feeling to a shared spiritual life.

To share one's spiritual life with others requires more than publicly praying with them, though shared prayer can be of great value and can be the beginning of shared spirituality. Shared spirituality moves beyond shared public worship and expressive prayer to the realm of friendship. If friendship begins when two or more persons discover that they share a common difference from others, a spiritual friendship takes root when a person realizes that someone else truly understands how important and central one's relationship with the holy is. Spiritual friendships can grow when the friends respect each other's spiritual sentiments, support each other's spiritual pilgrimages, and show loving care for each other's spiritual lives.

Spiritual friendship can be a dimension of the relationship shared among members of the same religious denomination. This happens when fellow believers have gone beyond the doctrine and moral teachings of their church or congregation and begin to share with each other the approach to the holy that underlies both doctrine and morality. Spiritual friendship can also be shared between and among members of different denominations of the same religion. A Catholic and a Protestant can learn about and respect the doctrinal differences that distinguish their respective ecclesial experience and expression of Christian faith. But they can also learn to understand, respect, and even envy each other's spiritual life, each other's approach to the holy as it has been informed by their church's tradition and theology. Ecumenical dialogue often stays on the level of doctrinal agreement or difference. Spiritual friendships among Christians from different denominations lead to a new experience of ecumenism, one that touches people at very deep levels.

Spiritual friendships can also develop between and among believers from totally different religions. Jews and Christians who share friendships in other ways can take their relationships to the levels of spirituality where they learn from and about each other's relationship with the Holy One. Muslims and Jews can and have crossed severe social, political, and religious divides to meet in spiritual friendship. So have Hindus and Muslims, Hindus and Buddhists, Buddhists and Christians, and so on. Even believers and those who are more agnostic about spiritual matters can meet in friendship to learn from each other about their ways to or detours around the holy.

Just as friendship is one of the great treasures of life, spiritual friendships are precious jewels in an increasingly diverse world where believers of all types regularly live and work together. Spiritual friendship does not discount the real differences between and among the friends, differences due to their religious and cultural backgrounds. Neither does spiritual friendship easily wave a magical wand of diversity to dismiss those differences. Such friendship respects and cherishes the other's spiritual pilgrimage, the other's sacred times and places, the other's images of God and relationship with the Holy One. Just as friendships take time to grow and develop, and require a commitment to continue, so also do spiritual friendships entail time, respect, and patience.

If our romances can tutor us in ecstasy, in the experience of stepping outside our self, to prepare us to meet the holy, then friendship can teach us that our spiritual lives need not be solitary. Even at the deepest levels of our souls, where we and our God meet, friends can be invited. Our spiritual pilgrimages can be shared with others we meet along the way.

Acquaintances

Romance comes and goes. Friendship is a great gift that comes to us on occasion, to be treasured and protected. Most of our lives, however, are filled with people with whom we are not in love and who are not close friends. They are acquaintances. English is less discriminating when it comes to distinguishing friends and acquaintances. We use the word *friend* to refer even to relationships that are not as deep and abiding as true friendships are. Other languages are more particular about who receives the title of friend. English seems overeager to bestow the more favorable term "friend" so as not to embarrass or offend the "mere" acquaintance.

Yet the truth is that if we were to list the people with whom we live, work, and play, few of them fit into the category of romance or friendship. They are simply there. We have been thrown together by birth into this family, by chance into this school, by fate into this job, by fortune into this religion. If our friends happen to share our daily lives, all the better, but most of the people we rub elbows with each day are acquaintances. Yet, we can exercise diligence among them just as well. Even without the fire of romance or the fervor of friendship, we can attend to our acquaintances with loving care, enriching them and ourselves in the process. We do not have any express commitment to acquaintances. Rather, we try to manage our lives and to do our work together with an easy and casual courtesy and respectful civility.

Acquaintances include our neighbors, our coworkers, our teammates and classmates, those who regularly deliver our mail and cash our checks, repair our cars and teach our children. They are the people with whom we share our daily spaces and tasks. Geographic proximity may be all that we have in common. We may like them, dislike them, wonder about them, and surprisingly miss them when they are no longer part of our lives. Even though they are not friends or lovers, we can grow amazingly fond of them.

In a way the members of our families fit into this category. One hopes that our spouse is the object of our romantic interest, and very fortunate husbands and wives will also cherish each other as friends. Parents and siblings, and eventually one's children can become one's friends. But the majority of our family members fit into the category of acquaintance, albeit very close acquaintances. They are the people with whom we shared the space of our homes as we grew up, or with whom we now live as family. They, too, are worthy of our diligence, our abiding love and care, despite their faults and limitations which time and proximity often magnify.

Our acquaintances, those in our families and those beyond the home, have something valuable to teach us. They tend to include many people who are very different from us, people we would never choose as friends, with whom we feel we have almost nothing in common. They would never interest us romantically, yet we must often work with them in consistently close quarters. Because many of our acquaintances are in fact so different from us, even contrary to how we define and understand ourselves, they serve as constant reminders of how limited we are, how narrow our interests and understanding, our experience and awareness really are. They confront us each day with who we are not, how we do not go about things, what we are not interested in, and why we do not live as they do.

The great variety of human choice and predicament that they represent puts our own individuality into bold relief. Our particular way of being human is, this great diversity reminds us, quite limited and peculiar to us. In reminding us of how people can be so different in so many ways, our acquaintances teach us about our limitations. They serve as sacraments of idiosyncrasy, bestowing on us the grace to recognize the right of others to be different, even profoundly different, from us. They also serve as constant invitations to diligence, that is, to loving care that is due even to those who do not warrant it by being our friend or lover, or by mirroring ourselves and our interests.

If we belong to a church or religious congregation, most of the others in the group will be acquaintances. As such, they will be different from us in many ways, even though we share a religious belief. Some may become our friends, even our spiritual friends, but most will not. They will stay on the periphery of our lives, challenging us to accept them as different from us and from each other.

This lesson of accepting differences, of extending diligence to those whom we would never choose as lovers or friends, is a very important one for the spiritual life. Encounter with the holy involves, above all else, a recognition of our limits, of our nature as creature, of our being given existence rather than originating it, of our limited sharing in the totality of being. Our acquaintances prepare us for this experience of limit and boundary. They help us accept the truth of how narrow our slice of life has really been; they tutor us in holy humility. Diligent love and care toward acquaintances is repaid many times over with the sometimes gentle, sometimes shocking reminders they extend to us of how singular, peculiar, and parochial we each are. That is an important lesson to take with us into our sacred times and places.

Sin and Diligence

Any study of diligence must deal with the topic of sin. One approach to sin, one way of framing it, is to consider the sinfulness that can be found in our relationships. All our relationships can be compromised and lessened by sin. There are the obvious offenses we commit against others. We betray our spouses in word and in action. We disappoint our friends by our failures to respond to their needs. We offend acquaintances by offhand remarks and casual insensitivity, even without meaning to hurt or ignore anyone.

Rather than count the many ways and means we sin against each other, we can focus instead on their commonality. Underneath all the visible fractures in our friendships, there is a hidden, unstable substratum that causes these surface failures. Hidden beneath the dangerous waves of a stormy romance or the sickly still sea of a stale marriage, there runs a dangerous current. Invisible in the thick air of hostility that surrounds resentful coworkers or divides distant, distrustful neighbors is a pervasive element that poisons the environment. The great variety of harms and misdeeds we can do to each other share a common denominator, something that we might say is the essence of relational sin. It is to treat another as an object.

To call something an object, or treat it as an object is to define it in terms of its use. Objects serve a purpose. They accomplish something for those who use them. Objects are tools that do work, instruments that secure an effect, aids for reaching a goal. Objects increase our power and magnify our efficiency. They extend our capacity to control, to investigate, to predict. Modern science, for example, depends on a great variety of tools and instruments. The scientist uses sophisticated equipment to explore and manipulate elements and forces in nature. The engineer applies many marvelous means to design and to make valuable products. When we know how to use tools, how to employ aids in our work, we can change the world for the better. Through the proper and educated use of objects, we can enrich human society and culture.

Difficulties arise when we use other persons as tools. Relational sin originates when we manipulate or control, employ or exploit another human being for our own self-centered purpose. We are not speaking here of the legitimate employment of workers, the dedication of labor to the production of goods. Relational sin is rather the intentional use of another—a beloved, a friend, an acquaintance—to procure something we think is good for us, despite its consequences for the other.

To do this, to use other people as objects, we have to deny them their interiority. To objectify other persons, either as individuals or as groups, we must strip them of their subjectivity, of their self-hood. We must divest them of their personal or social history, discard their self-image, and deflate their self-worth, disenfranchise them of their capacity to understand and choose. There are obvious and egregious examples of such objectification of others. The Holocaust, war, slavery, physical and sexual abuse, religious and social prejudice, and countless other forms of degradation attest to our uncanny and unconscionable ability to treat other human beings as objects to be used and discarded, rather than as subjects with souls. When we objectify an individual or a group, we exile them in the most radical way possible: from their own humanity.

Those who are sincerely interested in the spiritual life, who themselves have suffered personal or social exile, will presumably recoil from such objectification of other human beings. Yet, this tendency to objectify others, to use them to achieve some measure of control for our own purposes, is not always as obvious and evident as it is in the horrors of history or in the behavior of a sociopath. The objectification of another human being can creep into any of our relationships. In our romances, our friendships, and our acquaintanceships, we can shift all too easily from a respect for the other as equal to the use or abuse of the other as object. The shift can be imperceptible at first. We can move unawares from love to use, from respect to abuse.

To learn why and how we might so readily use others, we must consider our needs. It is our needs that lead us to treat others as objects, as tools to help meet or satisfy those needs. Of course, each of us brings a multitude of needs into every relationship. So much of the stuff of love and friendship is negotiating each others' needs, compromising, postponing, and substituting, so that we might help each other. There is nothing sinful in the diligent love of mutual attentiveness, of caring for our own needs and the needs of others.

However, we can lose this mutual attentiveness to each other's subjectivity. A particular need can overtake us. The other becomes less and less a subject to be encountered and more and more an object to be used. We can find ourselves relating to other persons almost exclusively because of what they offer us. We have objectified them and pushed them into exile.

There are people who unabashedly make use of others for their own sakes. This is the style of living, working, and playing that they have chosen. Such persons are to be found in all walks of life, all occupations, all nations, all cultures, and all religions. Those who are interested in spirituality are not as likely to be shameless users of others. Yet, the pursuit of the spiritual life does not immunize us against such use of others. Our many needs, especially ones of which we are not fully aware or to which we cannot admit, can still nudge us into relationships primarily for what the other may offer us. We can all too easily get stuck in that posture, unable to appreciate and affirm the other as subject. The reciprocal and mutual dimensions of the relationship can go unrealized, even unimagined. Our neediness as human beings, in all its various kinds and degrees, leaves us in a condition where we are always at risk of objectifying others. We too easily shift from mutuality to use of the other as object.

Sacred Space and Human Need

Relationship with God and an honest spiritual life cannot by themselves heal us of such need and such tendencies. However, when we make our personal pilgrimages, when we enter our personal sacred space, we have an opportunity to confront our own neediness. The quiet interiority of our sacred space can bring us face to face with our needs. In the precincts of our sacred time the power of those needs can manifest itself. The creative interiority of the spiritual life can help us plumb the depths of our needs, better understand the causes of our desires, unearth the roots of our wants. The more aware we are of the nature and origins of our needs, the less likely we are inadvertently to use another person in fulfilling them without due regard or respect for the other. The more honestly and authentically we have met our needs, the more care we can take in our relationships. To become a spiritual pilgrim is to accept one's own neediness as a constant companion along the pilgrim way. That willingness to recognize and honor our poverty of spirit, our incompleteness, helps us to remember and respect the subjectivity of others.

Sacred time and place not only provide an opportunity to face our own neediness; sacred space is also inherently hospitable. While we usually repair to our sacred spaces alone, retreating from our families and friends, the very interiority of sacred space is itself characterized by a certain attentiveness to others. Often this attentiveness to others begins as a felt presence of others in the midst of our sacred space. We may find that the image or voice of a particular person drifts into our sacred space. Or we may have a distant but distinct sense of someone's presence, or of the presence of several others. A truly sacred space is hospitable in these ways. Others become sharers in our retreats. They become present to us in deep and abiding ways. Our awareness of them and of their needs and concerns grows during the time we spend in our personal sacred place. We return to our busy lives more attentive to others, more attuned to their subjectivity, more diligent about their interiority. Because our sacred time and place is hospitable, we grow more sensitive to how our needs impact our relationships, more discerning about what behavior is respectful, encouraging, and life-giving.

The Greeks had a word to describe love: *agape,* which means "complete, total, unconditional, and undeserved love." The early Christians took this word and used it to describe God. The closest that the Bible ever comes to defining God is in the First Letter of John, where the author claims that God is love. John's letter, which was written in Greek, uses the word *agape* for love. "God is *agape,* and those who abide in *agape* abide in God, and God abides in them" (1 John 4:16).

We cannot know the full nature of God. We cannot idolize any one image of or idea about God. But we can with some certitude approach the holy, knowing that when we are in the divine presence, we are in the presence of absolute and infinite love, of *agape.* The spiritual life, then, can enrich and slowly transform all our relationships. The willingness to make sacred time and place a part of our lives, to go there often with humility and hope, can transform our relationships because it transforms us. By living more and more in the divine presence, holy love can work its way into our souls, healing our needs and wants, strengthening our capacity to love others for their own sake. As we come to know that all time and all places are sacred, we begin to realize that we live constantly in the presence of this redemptive divine love.

This healing process is never done. We never grow beyond need. As we age we may grow needy in new ways; or old familiar needs may return and persist. Our spiritual pilgrimage, however, can continually enrich our relationships. The endless love of the Divine One not only fills our sacred time and place; it spills over into our loves, our friendships, and our acquaintanceships. It slowly transforms all our relationships into ever more efficacious sacraments of love. It redeems us from our exiles.

CHAPTER 6

Loving Care for the World

There is a dichotomy that is sometimes part of a person's disaffection from religion and faith. It is the dichotomy between this world and the next. Religion and spirituality seem to be focused on the next world, on heaven, or on the "new heavens and new earth" one reads about in the Book of Revelations. Faced with a choice, many people choose to direct their energy and dedicate their work to this world. Whether or not they believe in a world to come, it seems to them irresponsible and escapist to set one's eyes on what is not yet and to ignore what is in front of us. There is so much here already that needs attention and improvement.

In fact, one can find much in religious literature and imagery that seems to relegate this world and its troubles to second-class spirituality. Monks or nuns whose attention is on God, on the soul, and on heaven are presumed to be more spiritual, holier, closer to the divine. There are prayers that bemoan our condition "in this valley of tears," that speak of our life on Earth as an exile, that describe our proper and true condition as pilgrims on this Earth with our final destination only in heaven. Indeed, for believers such language expresses truth and sets our present experience in the wider context of what God has prepared for us beyond death, beyond this present universe. For some people the pain and suffering they presently endure is made tolerable by their faith in something better to follow.

It does not follow, however, that faith and spirituality mean ignoring this world, its needs, and its challenges. Spirituality that snubs this world is not better or purer. It is not balanced. A difference between this life and a life to come does not necessarily mean a dichotomy. Just as we can understand and embrace our own self as God's gracious gift to us, so we can accept and welcome the world and all the universe as a divine bequest, meant for our loving care. The fullness of diligence includes creation, both the natural universe and the culture and society that has evolved from human gene and genius. Diligent involvement in protection of the environment and loving participation in the enrichment of society and culture can be holy catalysts for our spirituality. Properly practiced, the spiritual life does not counsel escape from the world, but a loving care for it.

A Spirituality of Creation

Pilgrimage to our sacred places and times can make us increasingly aware that all of time and every place are filled with the divine presence. As one stands before the Holy One, an awareness of the divine presence in and through all creation grows. God awaits us at the heart of creation, and invites us to cooperate in its transformation. Creation becomes understood as good, as the work of God, and as reflective or revelatory of God.

To experience a work of art is to experience the person of the artist. When contemplating a work of van Gogh, one can be transported by the painting into the artist's perspective on life. One can feel his delight or sense his pain. When listening to a symphony of Beethoven or a poem of Emily Dickinson, the angst and passion of the artist invade the soul. The artist's life and experience become real once again through the medium of the music or words. Even simpler works or crafts have this power to make their creator present. A piece of pottery made by a child in school reflects and carries much of the child's person, perspective, and concerns at that time in his or her life. A piece of furniture or other artifact made by loving hands carries that person's purpose and presence throughout time. We treasure such artifacts because they make their creator present to us.

The spiritual life brings a sense of creation as God's handiwork or artwork. One begins to see evidence of the divine purpose and presence throughout nature as well as in human culture. All of creation is affirmed as good, since it is from God and reflects God. In the first chapter of Genesis there is a litany affirming the goodness of creation. After each of the six days of creation, the text proclaims how God saw that what was created that day was good, very good.

There have been trends and movements, especially in Western Christianity, to withhold this affirmation of goodness from certain parts of creation. One persistent example of this selective affirmation of creation is the tendency to exclude the human body and to put it under suspicion. There are many reasons for this. Some pre-Christian cults, generally known under the name of "Gnostic," taught that the material world was not good, because it came not from God but from an evil source of some type or other. The Gnostics thought that spiritual reality was good, but the physical world was bad and could only get us in trouble. In the early years of Christianity, many converts came into the church from various Gnostic sects and brought their biases against the physical world with them. Soon some Christians were teaching that the physical part of the human person—the body—was not good and was, at least in some of its parts, the work of an evil being or force.

Unfortunately, this suspicion of the body and of its physical needs and desires came to dominate some traditions of Western Christian spirituality. To be spiritual meant to confront, conquer, and crush one's sexual feelings as well as one's other desires for comfort and enjoyment. Spirituality came to be synonymous with being otherworldly, with living like the angels who were pure spirit. This type of otherworldly religion, with its suspicions of the body and its contempt of our humanity, has sent many a believer into religious or even spiritual exile.

Certainly our sexuality can become unruly and destructive; many people have been the victims of unbridled sexual passion and exploitation. Likewise, the gratification of other bodily wants and needs has led to the treatment of persons and of nature as objects to be used for one's fulfillment. The power and persistence of the life forces within us should counsel care and even caution. However, to jump from such judicious counsel to the condemnation of our physical nature is to reject the joyful affirmations of Genesis. Indeed, throughout the Hebrew scriptures there is constant praise and celebration of human physicality and sexuality. Our bodies are also good, the work of God and reflective of God. A spirituality of creation needs to include *all* of creation.

Saint Augustine reflected on this dilemma. He accepted the truth of Genesis that all creation is good and the handiwork of the divine artist. Yet he knew, from his own experience, how human passion and feeling could lead to inappropriate use of other persons and of things. How does one affirm the being and goodness of all creation and yet account in a practical way for the human tendencies to misuse or even abuse other people or elements in creation? Augustine saw the answer in what he called "the ordering of love." Our stance or attitude toward all of creation should be one of admiring and even ecstatic love for the sheer beauty, complexity, and grandeur of it all. But it is a love that discriminates. Different elements in creation deserve different kinds of our love. We can love a flower, but not in the same way that we might love our dog. We can love our dog, but not in the same way that we love our friend. We can love our friend, but not in the same way that we love our God. Love discriminates. Diligence discerns.

To love is to affirm the being and goodness of someone or of something. The act of love is joyful acceptance that the other is. It is an acclamation that the other's existence is inherently good, an assent to their being. Since all things in creation have different ways of being, or different levels of being, we affirm their existence in proportion to their respective ways or levels of being. So when we love a flower, we affirm its being and all that characterizes its particular existence. Obviously a human being enjoys a whole different level and way of being. To love another person is a different kind of love, a whole different level of affirmation. Ordered loving, for Augustine, meant to love each being in proportion to its place in the great hierarchy of being. Trouble sets in when we get involved in "disordered" loving, when, for example, we love things more than living beings, or animals more than people, or people more than God.

We can preserve the ideal of loving all creation, of maintaining a profound diligence of the world, while making distinctions that reflect the variety in creation. Human sexuality is good and of God. Yet it is not to be valued more than other dimensions of the person. Sexuality should be loved in proportion to its relative place in the life, hopes, dreams, and promise of the beloved. In similar fashion, each aspect of creation is to be loved and respected in proportion to its place and purpose in all of being. Sacred time and place can provide the quiet reflection needed for the ordering of love. The practice of the spiritual life helps us reflect and realize a diligent order in the ways we relate to each other and to all the marvelous aspects of creation.

A Spirituality of Work

The work we do to make a living informs much of our relationship with nature as well as with society and culture. The effort and energy we expend in our occupation or profession impacts the world in many different ways. It is important, then, to see if and how our work might itself be an expression, in its own way, of loving care for the world.

Work can be characterized as diligent if it gives hope to other people and to the world. If what we do each day at the office or in the factory, in the field or in school helps to meet the legitimate needs of people, then it is a source of hope. If our work helps create implements and tools that build up society and advance civilization, then it is a source of hope. If our profession heals others, negotiates disagreements, forges alliances, and unlocks human potential, and helps to end exile, then it is a source of life. If our daily efforts assist others in the search for knowledge and understanding, if we inspire others to join in the transformation of society and in the appreciation of beauty, then our work is a source of ordered love. In these and many other ways our toil can be a continuous transformation of the world.

It is not only what we do that can inspire hope. *How* we do our work can also be transforming. The teachers who go about their profession with cynicism and reproach may actually betray their vocation and destroy the possibility of hope among the young. A machinist who plies his or her craft with loving skill can inspire others to equal diligence in their work. Our attitude, when it is one of loving care for what we do, is also vital. Living a spiritual life can make a significant difference in our attitude toward work.

Time spent in the presence of the holy can change the way we think about our occupations and professions. It can help us see our work in light of the sacred. The first comment on work in the Hebrew scriptures is to be found in the very first sentence of the Book of Genesis. God is described as being at work, creating the heavens and the earth. God's creative work is accomplished, according to the text, through a wind from God that swept over the face of the waters (Gen 1:1). The Hebrew word used here and translated as "wind" or in some English renderings as "spirit" is *ruah*. One of the many signs or symbols of the divine presence in both Hebrew and Christian scriptures is the mighty wind, the storm or tempest. God is also to be found in the gentle quiet, as we have seen in the story of Elijah the prophet who encounters God in "a sound of sheer silence" (1 Kgs 19:13). Or God can be found in the very breath of life, as in Genesis 2, where Adam, fashioned from the clay, becomes a living being when God "breathed into his nostrils the breath of life" (Gen 2:7).

The symbolic association of God's creative presence with wind, storm, breath, and silence expresses the Hebrew conviction that God is all around and within us, creating and recreating life in endless possibilities. To live the spiritual life is to immerse oneself consciously and continually in awareness and celebration of this divine Spirit. It is also to discover that the divine Spirit, once blown into the clay nostrils of Adam, is also within us. The spiritual life slowly reveals to us the truth that the Holy One, the divine creative Spirit who is everywhere, is also within us.

Our daily lives of work, then, can be more than a means of survival. They can even be more than sources of hope for others and for the world. The work we do can be a participation in the creative work of God. Just as God's Spirit moved over the waters in primordial creation, just as God's breath enlivened Adam and rescued Elijah and raised Jesus, so that same Spirit can work through us to continue the process and possibilities of creation. All diligent work can be understood as a vocation, a calling to participate as co-creators with the divine.

Unfortunately, for many people the reality may be quite different. Work may be drudgery that one loathes, a burden that one fears, an exile that one must endure. The place of one's work in society may deprive one of dignity and purpose. The lack of value ascribed to what one does can be dehumanizing for the worker. The tyranny of employers as well as the vagaries of the marketplace can all conspire to make work unbearable and even destructive rather than creative for the worker. In short, the nature or context of work can render the worker an object rather than a subject. It can deprive the workers of an interior life and discourage them from discovering purpose, meaning, or hope in what they do.

Such destructive social situations or economic systems need to be addressed and redressed. Issues of justice and liberation have to be confronted. However, one can engage simultaneously on a campaign of inner liberation. When finding oneself in a work situation that is not life-giving, one that objectifies and dehumanizes, a person can also reach into the soul for the resources necessary to confront problems and make changes. The spiritual life can become a resource for the oppressed worker. It can help one discover diligence in the present context as well as courage to change the situation in whatever ways are most creative for the individual and perhaps even for the society.

Our spiritual lives can also enrich and further culture by fostering a receptiveness and openness to the fruits of human ingenuity and creativity, to what others have wrought by their work. A loving care for the world offers hospitality to human resourcefulness and talent, thereby encouraging and furthering culture. Conversely our prayer and contemplation can be enriched by human culture. Works of art and literature, music and drama, science and philosophy may themselves be occasions that encourage and enhance our interior life. They themselves may in fact be sacred spaces for us, providing times and occasions that deepen our experience of the holy through our appreciation of human genius and its cultural and scientific expressions.

Diligence for the world also remains open to societies and cultures beyond our own. By calling us to deeper subjectivity, the spiritual life can broaden and deepen our appreciation of other cultures and what they may have to offer. Living a spiritual life can develop our hospitality to those who are different, who have different ways of organizing themselves and who express themselves, their hopes, and their dreams differently.

Spiritual hospitality for society and culture is not blind. It does not welcome indiscriminately all the things that society and culture have to offer. We can discern in our sacred space what is not so life-giving or what may even be hurtful and destructive. A spiritual life can help one be open to society and culture and at the same time be critical of them and consider them in light of the diligence and hope they inspire.

Diligence for the world sees traces of the Creator in all things. Everything is made to some extent in God's image and everything reflects the loving care of the divine artist. All creation attests to the diligence of the divine worker. In the same way, our work will leave traces of our effort, testimonies to our diligence, so long as we approach what we do with loving care. We become co-creators with the Holy One. Our image slowly merges with the divine image in creation as our work molds and shapes the world in ways that move it along its course toward fulfillment.

Nature: Subject or Object?

In chapter 5 we considered how we might treat other persons as objects, using them only to meet our needs. We can, of course, approach nature and the environment in the same way. We can consider other living species as well as the Earth and its resources as objects that are to be used in order to meet our individual and social needs. We may even go about this in a relatively responsible way, taking account of non-renewable resources, the needs of other peoples and nations, and other dictates of justice and prudence. Nonetheless, the objectification of nature and society rests ultimately on a model of study, control, and manipulation.

As creatures we are certainly dependent upon nature. We must use what our environment offers in order to survive and prosper, but there is another way to interact with the environment. This alternative approach does not rely solely or even primarily on the objectification of nature. Rather it recognizes our interdependence with the natural world and is based on an appreciation for and understanding of the world in its subjectivity.

It is not difficult to understand how we are to respect and respond to the subjectivity of other persons. Instead of viewing them as obstacles that impede our ends or as opportunities to aggrandize ourselves, we respect their rights as persons, we take account of their minds and hearts, their hopes and dreams. In short, to approach other persons as subjects is to take account of their interiority. But is it possible to approach nature as subject? Can one entertain any realistic notion of the interiority of the world and all its nonhuman creatures and resources? Isn't it just a romantic notion, a revival of the mythological personifications of animals, forces, and elements in nature, to speak of them as subjects?

One could argue that the subjectivity of many animals, especially of the higher animals, is not too difficult to entertain. Their sense perception, their social responsiveness and interaction, their capacity for pain and for play all appeal to our empathy and our imagination. As we have learned more about animal species, science has actually increased our understanding of and respect for their subjectivity. However, what of living creatures that are less like us? What of lower forms of animal life, of plant life, and of inanimate matter? How can we speak in any meaningful and instructive way about interiority when we refer to the vast multitude and variety in the universe?

One way to a spiritual appreciation of nature, to a meaningful regard for its interiority and subjectivity, is the way of complexity. When we objectify another human being we reduce him or her to one category of definition. Hitler decreed the Jews subhuman, and that category was used to justify all the horrors perpetrated on them. Serbian politicians categorize Bosnians as Muslim, and that one fact purports to explain and justify a war against them. A Protestant Irishman relates to a Catholic counterpart in one narrow religious role and ignores the rest of the person. Or vice versa. This reduction to one category, usually a category that conveniently justifies our ends, is the essence of objectification. To objectify someone is to consider him or her in light of one basic fact or fiction that is allowed to identify and define the person's totality. When we begin to consider people in all their complexity, the complexity of their inner life as well as the complexity of their social and familial roles, our tendency to objectify them gets stymied. We have to take account of them in light of the many truths about them. We have then to relate to them as subjects, not objects.

In the same way we can reduce all the beings, forces, or elements of nature to one category or other; we can exile them from their complexity. A forest can be seen simply as lumber to be harvested for gain. A mineral can be seen only as an energy resource. A species of animal can be reduced to its commercial use. But nothing in nature is rightly reduced to one category, nothing adequately appreciated by shrinking it to one unit of understanding. Every discrete unit in the natural world is within and of itself an immense complexity of interrelated components. Taken together, all beings and elements in the natural world, including ourselves, are interrelated with and interdependent upon each other. To objectify nature as a whole or in any one of its parts is to miss the most significant truth about its reality. To reduce nature or any part of it to one category and then to act on that reduction is to ignore or to compromise the complexity of created being itself.

Contemporary science has increased our knowledge and appreciation of the great complexities in nature. From subatomic particles to vast ecosystems, we have become more and more aware of the complexity and interrelatedness of elements in nature, from the simplest to the most evolved. The spiritual life can complement our scientific sophistication in this regard. For the spiritual life, as we have seen, increases awareness of and openness to interiority. Interiority, in turn, increases our capacity to entertain and respect complexity. As the spiritual life makes us more aware of our own inner complexity and that of other persons, it can also make us ever more perceptive of and responsive to the complexity in all of created being. A vibrant spirituality will make us uneasy about forcing any aspect of nature into one category, one unit of understanding.

Spirituality inspires a loving care for nature by deepening in the spiritual pilgrim a respect for and attentiveness to the complexities within all creatures and the interrelationships and many levels of complex connections among all realities. The irony is that our naïve objectification of forces and elements in the natural environment has in the end objectified us. Our imperial use and manipulation of natural resources has made us the object of reactions never predicted and consequences never imagined. Our own hubris even threatens to make of us exiles, resourceless refugees on a planet made desolate by our misuse of it. The spiritual life can help to redeem us. It can open us to more creative, sustainable, and life-giving ways of making use of the gifts of nature. In so doing it can help rescue us from the consequences of our dangerous objectification of nature.

Consumerism and Materialism

One of the ways we are defined in contemporary Western cultures is as consumers. Any one of us can be and frequently is reduced to that category and thereby objectified. Much money is spent on so doing. We are lectured day and night by commercial advertising about what and how much we need of a whole host of products. We are encouraged to buy and to use, to procure and to consume.

Of course, we need to consume; we need to use all sorts of things to survive. Problems arise, however, when we ourselves are summarily reduced to the category of consumer, when we are seen only as one who uses things up, when we are simply and solely encouraged to keep consuming at any cost. When so much of our waking life is monopolized to convince us that our first and proper nature is to consume, we begin to think of ourselves that way. We begin to treat ourselves as objects. We lose touch with our interiority.

One of the things that happens to us in sacred space is that we stop consuming. The nature of the quiet we experience in sacred time and place is that consumption slows down or stops. We turn down the volume or turn off the sounds that we regularly take in with our ears. We turn away for a while from the media feasts of sights and spectacles that both delight and distract us throughout the day or night. We may even find that fasting from food or drink, ceasing our consumption of them for certain times, can enhance our experience of the sacred.

To cease consumption in these and other ways is part of our experience of the quiet that sacred space offers us. In that quiet we learn to appreciate that we are more than just consumers. We become more discerning about the things we do want to consume: the sounds and sights, the food and drink, the products and goods. We can begin to simplify our lives by becoming more selective, discriminating consumers. A result of such discrimination is that we use less of the world's resources. We grow in solidarity with people from other societies, or with the refugees and exiles in our own midst, who have less in the way of material objects to begin with. We break the stereotypes of success and enjoyment that a consumer-oriented society forces upon us.

Closely related to consumerism is materialism, which is the accumulation of goods for their own sake and the valuing of these goods as measures of a person's worth. Materialism is the ethos that results from the attitude of consumerism. Materialism is based in doing and in having. Few things can short-circuit or short out an attitude of loving care for nature like materialism. It can lead to a completely utilitarian approach to both the natural and human environments, because the goal of materialism is to possess things for oneself. It does not ask questions about the effects of such possession on other persons, on social structures and situations, nor on natural resources. Together consumerism and materialism are the practical results of the objectification of nature and our environment.

Spirituality can be an antidote to materialism and consumerism. Living the spiritual life, making time for sacred time and space gives a person options to the habits of getting, having, and using. The spiritual can teach the simple joy of being. Sacred space slowly gives rise to a joy that comes through the humble and immediate experience of standing before the one who is the source of all that is. The spiritual life encourages satisfaction with the privilege of sharing existence with all other creatures.

Hope for Creation

Spirituality is not finally escape from the world, nor from work, nor from the commonweal. It is rather a deeper immersion, a baptism into creation, a confirmation of our stewardship for nature and culture. Sometimes the pilgrimages to our sacred places mean leaving behind our responsibilities for a while, and getting respite from our active, busy involvement, in order to refocus our vision and clarify our intention. Ultimately, however, we return, bringing the fruits of our contemplation with us to benefit our world.

The Christian Gospels are quite clear about this return to the world and about our responsibility for it. The main theme of Jesus' preaching was the kingdom of God. He went around announcing the end of things the way they were and the establishing of God's agenda for the world. He told his hearers that the messianic age was imminent, when God's creative power would once again move as a mighty wind over both human society and the natural world to transform everything. There were to be new heavens and a new earth. The oppressive structures and rulers of society would be deposed. God's will would be known and observed. Ordered love would bring all things to their fullness and completion.

The Jewish and Christian faiths, in particular, point to this messianic completion of creation. Both call their adherents to hope for and work toward it, to help heal the world, to end its exile from justice and peace. Diligence involves a call to be coworkers with the Holy One in the transformation of culture and of society, co-creators with God in renewing the Earth. A full and vibrant spirituality involves a life of diligent involvement in the divine destiny of the world.

Those who live this way become themselves signs of hope. Their respect for the complexity and interrelatedness of all creation inspires the same in others. Their careful and sparing use of things challenges others to examine their own habits of life. Their care for culture and concern for social structures become catalysts for creativity and change. Their passionate but ordered loving uplifts those who may have lost heart. Their work, intentional, focused, and formative, calls forth commitment from others. All such diligent habits become seeds of hope, strewn by God across the world.

PART THREE

Hope:
Investing in the Future

*Hope and the kind of thinking that goes with it
cannot submit to the reproach of being utopian,
for they do not strive after things that have "no place,"
but after things that have "no place as yet,"
but can acquire one.*
Jürgen Moltmann, *Theology of Hope,* Introduction

J ust as exile is a crisis in love, it is also a crisis in hope. Hope is our attitude toward the future, our willingness to get involved in the future by investing our heart and soul in the present. Hope is our readiness to work on what will be, to prepare it as a gift to be left for those who follow us, who will inherit the Earth from us.

When we have suffered an exile of some type, our attitude toward the future, our willingness to get involved in the present, our readiness to leave any legacy is seriously compromised. How can we trust the future when we have just lost the past? How can we invest ourselves in anything when we have been ourselves divested, when circumstances or decisions have deprived us of what is dear? Indeed, exile can easily lead toward despair.

For the displaced believer, religious exile or spiritual exile raise particular problems around hope. How can one claim hope when faith itself is in question? Where do we look for hope when we can't find faith? Upon what might we found our hope when all our religious or spiritual foundations have been shaken or have crumbled?

It is when the exiled person becomes a pilgrim that hope begins to return. When we begin to set aside sacred space in our lives, we are also making room for hope. Hope, like diligence, can slowly emerge amidst the quiet interiority of our sacred times and places. When we take care to visit our sacred space, we are in fact investing in the future, not only in our own future, but also in the future of others, of the world. By living the spiritual life we affirm the future of all life. By embarking on the spiritual pilgrimage we invite others to consider the possibilities of new life and new hope that await us down the road. The spiritual pilgrim is really an exile who travels forward in hope.

When we hope we are not alone; hope is by its very nature shared with others. Because it is never solitary, hope calls us out of exile, out of our separation and alienation. It unites us with others in our common vision of and work for the future; or it unites us with those yet to come for whom we work. Effective hope involves some level of commitment to others, working with or for them on the future. Hope is our common response to what we together believe is possible. It is our willingness to stay together in order to realize those dreams.

The exile, however, does not grow into hope easily. It is born of much suffering, of much dying and rising again from the dead. It requires of us many conversions, radical changes in the ways we think, in how we construct our values, and in how we expect God might be involved in our building the future. Hope is finally, some would attest, a work of grace, of God's willingness to join us in our commitment to the future.

CHAPTER 7

Grace

T he subject of grace can drive people away from institutional religion. They may not use the word or be familiar with the theology, but grace is at the heart of their disaffection. It has to do with what we might call the "rights to" grace, or the "patent on" grace.

Most believers presume that they must earn, gain, or somehow merit grace. Be good, God will repay you with grace. Go to church and worship, you will get grace. Give generously to the poor and needy, God will reward you with grace. In this approach, religion is tit for tat. Grace is a commodity or a benefit one receives for some investment or other. And the church controls all the assets. In the Middle Ages the church even began to keep something like investment portfolios on grace, accounting for how much grace one received for this or that outlay of time, prayer, fasting, or almsgiving. Indulgences were sold according to allotments of grace prescribed for various kinds of good works and religious deeds. In such an approach grace is seen as a supernatural thing or substance that one receives from or through the church. It is cashed in at death, and we begin an eternity of deferred benefits. If we are in arrears, we may or may not be able to arrange a payment program.

Such an approach to grace can drive people away from religion. They may simply despair of being able to keep to the regimen required to receive grace. They may feel like failures at worship or good works, and conclude that they do not qualify for God's grace. So they give up on religion. Others are simply offended that any institution might presume to have the rights to or patent on something as precious and essential as God's grace. They hold religion in contempt because of its presumption or its hypocrisy. They choose religious exile rather than be complicit in such a sacred scheme. Still others dismiss any theology that concretizes grace, that makes of it a kind of supernatural substance or benefit, as if anyone could divide and measure divine love.

Closer, careful thinking about grace suggests that it is not and could never be earned. Grace is not a reward, a payment, or compensation. It is not a thing at all. Grace is God's free and totally unconditional gift of love. It is God's *agape* in action. People are saved because God has graciously forgiven all their sins and called them into a loving relationship. If one is ethical and moral, it is part of a grateful response to God's initiative and a result of living in union with God, not a prerequisite. We experience grace when we feel and accept God's forgiveness, when we hear and respond to God's invitation to live in the divine presence, and when we begin to experience the fruits of such a life.

Grace and the Spiritual Life

If grace is not a reward one gets for being good or prayerful, then how does it fit into the spiritual life? We can turn from the image or model of grace as a supernatural reward that one receives in various quantities for different feats or fasts, to some alternative models or images. No one image or model will be perfect. Each has advantages and disadvantages in trying to reach a better understanding. There are three models that, taken together, may provide some helpful insights into the role of grace in our spiritual lives. Each of these models is a way of understanding the spiritual life itself and how grace may be a part of it.

The first model is that of *pilgrimage*. We have used it before to speak about sacred space. A pilgrimage, as we have employed the image, is taking the opportunities to enter the times and places that are sacred to us. Pilgrimage, however, can be expanded to be a paradigm for the spiritual life itself. The spiritual life, as we have defined it, is a daily reflection on our relationship with the Holy One and a consistent attempt to work that relationship into all aspects of our life. This whole way of living can itself be considered as a pilgrimage, as an intentional journey on the way to meet God.

To think of the spiritual life as a pilgrimage has implications for the way we understand and explain spirituality. If the spiritual life is a pilgrimage, then it is something that continues. We are always on the way, never arriving. If we use the model of pilgrimage for the spiritual life, then the scenery and landscape, the byways and crossroads are always changing. We may stop and rest awhile, but we inevitably have to get moving again onto the next stage of our journey. This is all quite different from thinking of the spiritual life as a state, even as a "state of grace," as religious literature often calls it. To be in a state is to be stationary, arrived and completed, whole or saved. It is a very different image of the spiritual life and expresses a very different experience.

If the spiritual life is seen as a journey, then how might we see the idea of grace in that image? There are several ways. One is to ask why a person has set off on this spiritual pilgrimage to begin with. Where did the idea come from and why does one keep going? Somehow, at some time, perhaps in the midst of religious or spiritual exile, the pilgrim received some kind of invitation or call. Pilgrims are on the way to somewhere they hold to be important. Some kind of summons or incitement got one to make the decision and start the journey. For the spiritual pilgrim, that call is from God, from the Holy One. Each pilgrim may hear it in different ways, receive it in different forms, but it is always from God. This divine invitation is grace. The initiative to respond to the invitation is grace; and the courage to continue to respond is grace.

Following the spiritual pilgrimage month after month, year after year, can become tedious. One might be tempted to give up the quest and go back, or go anywhere else but the spiritual route. The strength we need to keep going, the energy and recommitment to continue the journey is grace. The people we meet who encourage us, the spiritual food they give us, the rest and restoration we get from joining other pilgrims at various wayside inns: it is all grace.

As we travel further and further along our pilgrimage, our legs get stronger, our energy increases, and we can make far longer daily distances than when we first began. That increase in spiritual endurance and strength is grace. The keenness of observation and the wiliness of the seasoned traveler that we acquire along the way are grace. All that we learn about the destination of our pilgrimage, about the one we hope some day to reach is grace. And the one toward whom we travel is grace. If the spiritual life is a pilgrimage, then the grace of God's infinite love fills every aspect of that pilgrimage; it inspires and empowers us to go on, from the very beginning to the very end.

A second image we can use to understand the spiritual life is that of an *excavation*. We can think of the spiritual life as an archeological dig, a sustained and careful search for something of great value that is hidden but real, a buried treasure that is the reason, meaning, and purpose for one's digging.

In this model, grace is the first hint or suspicion that indeed something of great value is to be found here, in this place. Grace is the knowledge of times and cultures past or of rediscovered clues in the present, the ability to read the landscape for evidence and indications that this is the spot to begin to dig. Grace is also the knowledge and skill to know *how* to dig. It is the ability to unearth the treasure without harming or destroying it. Grace is the ability to work with the many others who are necessary for the success of your excavation. It is your appreciation of the expertise of others and of their dedication and passion for the work.

Grace is also the thrill of discovery, not just the final unearthing, but each little confirmation that one is digging in the right spot, in the right ways, with the right instruments. Grace is the uncovering of the treasure of divine love, and grace is the treasure itself. In this model, grace is all that initially inspired and all that keeps us going, until we arrive at that which has been hidden from ages past but is now revealed.

A third model for understanding the spiritual life is that of *scientific inquiry* or quest. Scientists study, research, and experiment for many reasons. It may be to discover a particular object or entity, such as a specific gene or chromosome, a subatomic particle or wave, a species of insect or cure for a disease. Or the quest may be for a theory that elegantly unites and explains the disparate data about a phenomenon.

The spiritual life, especially for those people who value scientific ways of study and investigation, can be like a scientific quest. Only it is a search not to explain how, but *why:* a search not for causes but for meaning. If the spiritual life is viewed as a scientific quest, then grace is the initial suspicion or intuition that one had which then inspired the quest. Grace is the skill and ingenuity one uses to follow this set of assumptions, this pattern of relationships, these bits of evidence. In this image of the spiritual life as scientific inquiry, grace is the curiosity that drives one on and the passionate thirst to know and know as fully as possible. In considering the spiritual life as a scientific quest, grace is the thrill of confirmation and the pure joy of discovery.

The spiritual life can be imaged or modeled in many other ways as well. Each model or paradigm that one uses to gain more understanding of the spiritual life and its dynamics will reveal different aspects and give different insights into spirituality. No one model is sufficient; all models have their limitations and foreclose certain perspectives. The point here is that when it comes to the divine, to the Holy One, everything is received, nothing is merited. Our spiritual lives are not our inventions. They are inspired, from their very inception, by grace, by the holy approaching us in a myriad of ways, most of which we are not even aware at the time. Our spiritual life is in every way a work of grace, a result of God approaching, coaxing, empowering, threatening, prodding, pushing, calling, and loving us in a thousand different ways so that we but respond. Even that response is a work of grace, a result of the Holy One surging in and through our very ability to approach the divine who comes to us.

God and Grace

Just as there are different models that can be used for understanding grace, so too there are different ways of thinking about God. Two seemingly contradictory ways present themselves. One way is to understand God to be out there, distant, somewhere else. In this approach, which emphasizes God's transcendence, the divine is thought about as totally different from, above, and beyond human reality. The second way is to understand God to be within, present in, and through us. This way of speaking about God dwells on divine immanence, on the presence of God within human experience, within the mysterious depths of our soul. Both of these approaches, like the images and models we used for the spiritual life and grace, are metaphors. When we speak of God, we always speak in metaphors, not in immediate, descriptive language. Both of these metaphors— God as out there and God as within—name some truth. Neither is complete or capable of naming the whole truth about the divine presence. Each forecloses many other understandings. Yet each approach can help us think about our relationship with God.

Both ways of speaking about God are found in the Bible. In the Hebrew scriptures there are passages that allude to this understanding of God as dwelling within us, as immanent. God's law, the great

Torah, is understood to have come from God and to carry with it the divine presence. This sacred law is described in the Book of Deuteronomy as dwelling within the person. "It is not in heaven, that you should say, 'Who will go up to heaven for us, and get it for us so that we may hear it and observe it?' Neither is it beyond the sea, that you should say, 'Who will cross to the other side of the sea for us, and get it for us so that we may hear it and observe it?' No, the word is very near to you; it is in your mouth and in your heart for you to observe" (Deut 30:12–14). The law and its divine author are within, waiting to be recognized and acknowledged.

In the New Testament there are also numerous places where the authors speak of God dwelling within the person. Saint Paul tells the Christians in Rome that their behavior needs to be radically different from that of those around them because "You are in the Spirit, since the Spirit of God dwells in you" (Rom 8:9). He also writes about "this mystery, which is Christ within you, the hope of glory" (Col 1:27). And as we have seen in 1 John, God as unconditional love, as *agape,* is acclaimed as dwelling in the person who also loves. "No one has ever seen God; if we love one another, God lives in us, and his love is perfected in us….God is love, and those who abide in love abide in God, and God abides in them" (1 John 4:12,16).

We find this emphasis on interiority in many other spiritual writers as well. In his *Confessions,* Saint Augustine writes about his religious conversion. Speaking to God he says, "Late have I loved you, Beauty so ancient and so new, late have I loved you. Lo, you were within, but I outside, seeking for you there, and upon the shapely things you have made I rushed headlong, I misshapen. You were with me, but I was not with you" (*Confessions,* Book X, 38). Elsewhere Augustine expresses his belief in the divine indwelling with the phrase, "God is more intimate to me than I am to myself."

Saint Theresa of Avila, a sixteenth-century Spanish nun and mystic, spoke about the presence of God within using the image of the castle. She invites us to think of our souls as one of the many castles that graced the hills of her native Spain. The spiritual life is taking time to visit the castle that is one's own soul. There are many apartments and rooms in the castle, just as there are many spaces and dimensions of our soul. As we explore our castle we eventually discover an interior garden in the middle of the castle. When we finally go there, we discover that the Lord has been sitting there all along, in that sunny, interior garden, waiting for us.

There is great comfort and hope in this mystery of God within. The believer who is removed from religion, thrown into doubt about faith, may draw inspiration and courage from these testimonies of scripture and saints. God goes into exile with the displaced believer because it is in the hidden depths of our humanity that the mystery of God dwells. Cult and creed, fellowship and service may have been left behind; God cannot be so easily shaken off.

This approach to the divine mystery helps us also think about the role of religion. Those entrusted with leadership in the church have the responsibility to preach and teach this good news about the Holy One who dwells within, to call people to discover and celebrate that gift of the Divine Creator, made manifest in Christ. Each human soul touches, in its depths, the mystery of the Divine Being. Religious faith is our response to the revelation of our true identity as God's image. Grace is both God's gift of the divine indwelling and all that brings us to that truth.

The metaphor of divine transcendence, of God as totally different from and completely beyond our human categories and experience, is also found throughout scripture. It appears early on, when after their expulsion from Eden Adam and Eve no longer enjoy the daily companionship of God. They and their descendents suffer alienation from God. It is found throughout the books of the prophets, who bemoan Israel's infidelity and godlessness, and constantly proclaim God as "holy," which meant shrouded in mystery beyond what mortals could ever attain or even imagine. It pervades Israel's hope for a Messiah who would come and restore God's kingdom in the fallen world. In the Christian scriptures God's transcendence is also expressed. Jesus preaches the kingdom of God amidst a world full of evil and evildoers. The pervasive power of evil in the world and in human hearts emphasizes a world and a humanity bereft of God and of grace. In this view only faith in Christ can put people right and set them on the road to salvation.

Religion in this understanding is the divine call to forsake a godless world and to accept God's grace so that it might transform and renew our minds, hearts, and souls. The church has been entrusted with the good news of God's forgiveness in Christ. Until we respond and accept that gospel, we are far from God, lost and adrift in a world that does not recognize the truth. Only grace, God's forgiving and loving approach to us in our sin, can turn us toward our proper destiny. In this understanding of God as totally above and beyond our human nature, what is within our souls is a deep hunger for God, a yearning for the divine, a vacuum and emptiness that only God can fill. In our confused human sinfulness we try to fill that vacuum with all sorts of things, none of which can satisfy our deep longing for the divine.

God as transcendent helps us understand those who suffer profound spiritual exile. For some people the spiritual life may feel more like a lament for an absent God, for a God who seems to exist beyond the mountains and far away across the sea on which they are presently quite lost and drifting. There may be times when the metaphor of God within seems nothing more than metaphor, and the holy is mysterious precisely because it is so absent, remote, and inaccessible. Certainly for some people it seems that God cannot be with us or within us. Or if so, then the divine is hidden so deep that no amount of excavation will ever get to the bottom, no pilgrimage will be long enough to arrive at its end, and no search so sustainable that it will ever resolve in discovery.

There is no easy answer for spiritual pilgrims who feel this alienation from God so deeply. One cannot dismiss their disaffection or even their despair with easy explanations about grace. If they persist in the conversation, however, there is one place where believer and doubter can still meet. It is at the point of sacred time and sacred place. Even if the divine seems distant, distracted, and absent, the spiritual seeker can still be a pilgrim. Even in our moments or years of disengagement from the divine, we can continue to go within, to experience inner quiet and joy, to treasure the ones we love within the embrace of that interior affection. Though the divine may offer only a "sound of sheer silence," as in the experience of Elijah, the pilgrim may find in that silence the seeds of a transformation of the human and of its transcendent possibilities.

The God as immanent approach is often identified with Catholic theology and spirituality, while God as transcendent is seen to characterize Protestant thought and experience. In fact, believers of all denominations use both ways of thinking about God to reflect on their own religious experience at different times in their lives. Believers displaced from all sorts of religious communities can name or describe their religious and spiritual struggles by considering these two metaphors. What is certain is that both of these images of God, as within or as beyond, are themselves gifts of grace, promptings from this God we presume to think about, this God who coaxes and cajoles us in every possible way to accept infinite love.

Grace and Sin

There is an ancient Hindu parable that tells about a man who was having a nightmare. In his disturbing dream he has lost his beloved wife. He runs frantically up and down the darkened streets of the city, desperately searching for the woman, who is nowhere to be found. He grows more and more anxious, his breathing gets shallow, and his heart is pounding. Suddenly he awakes from the dream. Coming to his senses he realizes that it was all a dream and that his wife is sleeping peacefully beside him. Hindu teachers use this parable to inform their students about the true nature of our souls. We search for God, for *brahman,* frantically looking outside ourselves, sometimes getting anxious and fearful, other times losing hope and giving up. All the while, says the Hindu sage, the transcendent is within us.

Another parable tells of the lion cub who, separated from its den, wandered into a flock of sheep. There it was raised as if it were one of the lambs. It grew up unaware of its true nature. The soul is like the lost lion, living as if it were something or someone other than who it truly is. A third Hindu story is similar. A prince was hunting alone when he fell from his horse and suffered a blow to his head that caused amnesia. Since he was in hunting costume, his clothing gave no clue as to his royal identity. He wandered around his own kingdom not knowing who he was or where he belonged. So too, we human beings can wander through life unaware of our true identity, not knowing that we are made to carry the mystery of the Holy One within us.

The Hindu parables can serve to remind all spiritual seekers that they can be like the dreaming husband, the displaced lion, or the amnesiac prince. We can forget who we truly are, beneficiaries of the divine affection that approaches us. We can go through life living in a kind of dream state in which we remain unaware of reality, namely, of the reality of grace. This unawareness, this forgetfulness is a basic alienation from our identity and our destiny. This alienation can be thought of as sin. It is not sin in the sense of evil acts committed or of good acts omitted. It is more like the Christian teaching of original sin, of a sinful state inherited, of a condition for which we are not responsible but which has a definite impact on us day in and day out. Such original forgetfulness can lead to a lifestyle of alienation from oneself and from others, as well as from God. Forgetting about grace, or ignoring its invitation, leaves us prone to deepen this original alienation by acts that further divide us from our self and from others.

Grace is the divine invitation extended to us in our state of alienation, in our forgetfulness about our true nature and destiny. Grace is God approaching us despite our willful acts that work more alienation into our lives and into the lives of others. Grace is the healing power of the holy seeking to mend the broken relationship with our inner self. It is the holy calling us into divine relationship through our inner self.

When we respond to the initiatives of divine grace, when we begin to make our little pilgrimages to sacred space each day or week, we begin to wake up. Like the sleeping husband, we shake off our night terrors and slowly begin to focus on what the truth is. Like the lion and the prince we begin to discover our true identity. Grace and the spiritual life do not guarantee that we will be sinless. We continue to struggle with the forces of alienation. We continue to lapse into forgetfulness. But grace and the spiritual life can slowly help us live more and more out of the truth of who we are and for whom we have been made. They can slowly mold our characters and our lifestyles to reflect that truth, and in so doing make us occasions of grace for others.

The Role of Religion

Just as we can think in different ways about grace and about God, so too we can consider religion from many points of view. It can be helpful for someone who struggles with the role and meaning of religion to step back and apply different models to it. The three different metaphors that we have used for the spiritual life can also be applied to institutional religion.

If, for example, we take spirituality to be a pilgrimage, then religion can be understood in several ways. We can think of the congregation or other members of the church as fellow pilgrims with whom we share the journey. Enjoying camaraderie and fellowship, we support, encourage, and challenge each other along the pilgrimage. Religion is also the holy hospitality and sacred meals we take together to strengthen us for the journey. Religion is an expression of our commitment to the journey and our pledge to help others along the way.

If we understand the spiritual life to be like an excavation, then religion is the wisdom of all the diggers who have preceded us. It is the learned skills and patient observations, the maps and soundings produced by our forebears in the faith that have led us to this one spot. It is reading about and sharing in their work, their discoveries, their finds, and being inspired.

If the spiritual life is like a quest for scientific knowledge, then religion is the discipline that enables us to frame the questions and design our hypotheses. It offers us language we can use to speak about God with our fellow seekers, and in which we can express our findings. It is the ways and the willingness to doubt, to wrestle with life's questions, and to struggle to articulate, if not final answers, at least formulas that keep us open and expectant to God's unfolding truth.

These, at least, are ways of thinking about how religion can help us along the pilgrim path. The reality, however, can be quite different. Institutional religion has often failed in its mission. The metaphor of God as transcendent is instructive here. We often think of the church or any religious institution as the place where God dwells. God, we presume is present, if not in a building or temple, then in the community of believers and worshipers. Yet, the scriptural tradition that reminds us of God's holiness, of the absolute otherness and remoteness of God, can also be applied to religious institutions such as the church. The church, both in its individual members and in its corporate identity, insofar as it fails in its mission, is bereft of God. To the extent that it is sinful, oppressive, abusive, judgmental, and prejudiced, the church no more has God at its center than does any other human institution. Even at its best, the church cannot presume to contain or corral God. The divine mystery is totally above and beyond what the church could ever embrace.

Yet, the metaphor of the divine indwelling also applies to the church. The immanent God, present in the depths of the human soul, is also present in human community, especially in those communities of faith that strive to understand and celebrate this mystery. In this approach God's presence fills the community of believers, their gatherings, their symbols, and their worship, despite their sinfulness. Jesus' promise always to be with his followers affirms this. When the church sins it does not abrogate God's presence; it rather betrays that presence. When the church fails its members and those who search for light and meaning, it acts as though God were not present within its word and sacrament.

It is the presence and power of God's grace that saves the church, often enough from its own failures. God permeates our lives with so many expressions of divine love, with ever-unfolding opportunities to respond. In the same way the church receives divine help and strength to carry on its mission to preach the gospel. Yet, just as we often fail to recognize and accept grace, so too does the church fail us. The one cause for hope amidst our individual and institutional failures is grace.

CHAPTER 8

Conversion

I t may sound odd to call a person's quarrel with organized religion a conversion. We usually speak of a person converting *to* a religion, not moving away from it. This common understanding of conversion as joining a religion or changing one's religious affiliation is not, however, the only understanding of the word. There is another way of defining conversion.

Conversion, in the wider meaning of the word, can be understood as "any significant, irrevocable, and radical change in a person's life." Every day of our lives we go through many changes. Physically, intellectually, socially, spiritually, we are constantly adjusting, modifying, transforming, switching, and shifting in ways of which we are sometimes aware and sometimes unaware. Many of these changes in the ways we think or feel or choose are not of great import. They are more accidental variations, more like moving the furniture around. Other changes carry much greater import for us. If we lose our home, for example, something more significant than redecorating has happened: something substantial, and with serious implications. We can call these more substantial changes "conversions." When we find ourselves in religious or spiritual exile, a substantial change in our life has occurred. We have experienced a conversion in the broader sense.

These types of conversions, these substantial changes in our lives, are irrevocable, that is, we cannot go back on them. Even if we do try to restore things to the way they were, it can never be as if we hadn't gone through the change. That little bit of our history cannot be denied and deleted. Conversion is also a change that is radical. It is not a surface or superficial difference; it goes to the root of our person or of the situation we are in. Finally, a conversion is a significant change, that is, it carries meaning and import for who we are, how we think about ourselves, how others see us, and how we relate to the world.

Our lives are full of conversions, of changes that are significant, irrevocable, and radical. From the choice of a mate to the choice of a career, we make decisions and selections that impact our lives profoundly and on many different levels. The decisions or changes that concern the role of religion or spirituality in our lives are substantial ones. The displaced believer, who decides to leave the religion that has been home since childhood, undergoes a significant, irrevocable, and radical change. Such a decision makes a significant difference in the believer's spiritual biography and in the web of his familial and social relationships. Its effects go to the very roots of a believer's faith and spiritual life, indeed, to the roots of her very sense of self. Even if the person decides to return at a later point to his or her original faith community, the time spent in religious or spiritual exile still makes an irrevocable difference. It cannot be wiped from the slate.

To think of our religious and spiritual struggles as conversions puts them in a new light. We usually think about our doubt and disappointment with religion in negative or pessimistic terms. To use the word *conversion,* to reflect on our religious or spiritual pain as significant, irrevocable, and radical change, allows us to consider how God might be involved in the experience. The word *conversion* also suggests that one is turning toward something new and compelling. We can also parse the word to take a closer look at the various ways in which we change during our religious or spiritual exiles.

All such changes, however, can be very difficult and demanding. They can involve a sometimes traumatic letting go, a kind of dying to the past and to what has been. A look at conversion will show that it is indeed a kind of death as well as a coming through to new life.

Death and Dying

So often in life we have to leave what is familiar and comforting to us. When we moved from one neighborhood or town to another as a child, when our family was broken up by separation or divorce, when we graduated from school, when we lost a job or ended a relationship: in these and a thousand other ways we have all come to experience separation from the familiar. Such separations usually mean that we must also face the unknown. All of these situations involve not only being separated from what is familiar, comfortable, and known, they also baldly confront us with the unknown. What is the new neighborhood or school going to be like? How will I survive without my job; how will I support myself and my family? What will life be like without my spouse or without my children? How can I leave this group of friends or companions who have so filled my life with meaning and joy? What lies beyond?

At the time of such significant separations, the future can look very dark and indistinguishable, affording no glimpse or clear view as to what lies ahead. When we go through such difficult separations, not only do we face the unknown; we are also not in control of our destiny. We would not have allowed this to happen if we had some measure of control, or we would not have let it happen in this way. Forces and persons beyond our influence are calling the shots. We cannot fight the riptides and undertows that pull us where we do not want to go.

Any life situation or circumstance that fits the description of these three dynamics is a kind of death experience. Any time in our lives when we are separated from what is familiar, faced with the unknown, and unable to control and determine what is happening, we are in a way dying. Physical death may also, to a limited extent, be described by these three dynamics. At the end of our years we must leave behind all we have known and loved, we face the absolute unknown, and we surrender control. What we might be able to say about the experience of bodily death comes from the many rehearsals throughout our lives, when we do indeed die a thousand deaths in life.

The substantial changes that we have called "conversions" more often than not involve some dying, some separation, some anxiety about what is to come, some surrender of control. Certainly every exile, be it personal, social, political, religious, or spiritual, is a death experience. The displaced believer, who chooses or is forced to leave his or her religious home, suffers a dying process. The spiritual exile, who feels godforsaken amidst the absurdity of life, has suffered a real death.

Resurrection

We do not know what lies beyond physical death. However, we do know what it is like to go through a dying process that is part of our life experience. We did survive the move to a new neighborhood as a child. We met new friends, our horizons were broadened, and we learned a lot about ourselves in the process. We did get through the trauma of separation and divorce. We may have come apart and fallen to pieces, but somehow we got put back together again. Life may even be much better than it was. We left the school that once was our whole world to discover a much wider world with many more opportunities than we imagined. We have negotiated the layoff or the firing, even if not graciously or courteously. We moved on to a new place or a new career and were the better for it.

In all such circumstances and many others like them, we faced the unknown and went right smack into it. We let go and surrendered control, because we had no other choice, really. And still we came through it. This is how we might understand resurrection, as a coming through death to a new life. It is not a cheating of death, not a pseudo-dying, not an end run around the dying process. Resurrection can be described as going through the separation, facing the unknown and losing control, but then emerging on the other side—changed. After dying, after going through the pain and trauma involved in a dying process, we come to a new experience of life, to a fuller, broader, deeper, and wider capacity for living.

In the Hebrew scriptures the word for "life" is *chai*. It does not mean simply a living, breathing, reproducing creature, as distinguished from an inanimate object. *Chai* means "more." It means openness to and hunger for all that the world and life and others have to offer. It is a passion for experience, a deep-rooted desire to take in as much as we can, not as consumers who devour, but as connoisseurs who practice the arts of living with gusto and gratitude. Resurrection means more of *chai*. It means that we have come through a dying process, and as a result we have a greater capacity for life. We can receive more of living.

One could also argue, or testify from personal experience, that this rising process is not guaranteed. Sometimes the dying–rising process gets short-circuited and is not completed. Sometimes the person breaks down midway and just cannot go on. Certainly there is much evidence for such breakdowns and mishaps. A divorce can leave a person doubting his or her capacity for intimacy for the rest of life, never allowing another to get close again. The loss of a job can lead to despair, to giving up altogether. The loss of bodily control brought on by a disease can lead to a loss of all hope for the future. This business of dying and rising is tricky and fraught with danger. The doubter might say that those dying processes that do not lead to new and fuller experiences of life are also candidates for suspecting what might or might not happen in physical death.

The question of life, or more accurately of unimagined and undreamed of *chai,* after physical death, is one of the most poignant religious or spiritual questions there is. It is ultimately a question of faith, of how one chooses to interpret our shared human experience and its future possibilities. In Christianity the resurrection of Jesus and the assurance given to believers that they will share in his victory over death are central to the faith (Rom 8; 1 Cor 15).

What is certain, however, is that significant, irrevocable, and radical changes in our religious and spiritual lives involve a dying process; and often they hold out hope for new life as well. In the midst of religious or spiritual exile, we can undergo conversion; we can experience substantial change that enriches and enlivens us in new and unexpected ways. Though difficult, such conversion can be an affirmation, a clear choice and confirmation of the new life that one has discovered beyond dying. Conversion can be a celebration and a salutation of the *chai* that newly fills one's mind and heart.

Intellectual Conversion

There are different types of conversion, of substantial life changes we might consider. One is intellectual conversion. This involves the move to a new way of understanding things, a new paradigm or philosophy that we use to make sense of the world and of our experience in it. We consciously abandon an old model that helped us negotiate our way in the past. We take on a new model. One might think of the conversion from a liberal political philosophy to a more conservative one. In the past, liberal ideas, policies, philosophy, and practices might have been the lenses through which one interpreted and evaluated social and cultural experience. Becoming more conservative or more liberal is an intellectual conversion, because one exchanges the basic assumptions about what is good and helpful for individuals and society.

Another kind of intellectual conversion can happen when we move from one culture to another. The new culture in which we come to live usually offers all sorts of new ways of thinking about life, politics, religion, and other people. The change to a new culture also involves a dying process, because so much of what we took for granted as the best ways of interpreting the world is now challenged by what is considered best in our new culture. Negotiating such a change is not easy. One can, however, actually come to adopt the predominant outlook and bias of one's new place. This is intellectual conversion, all the more convincing if one is intentional and informed about the change of perspective.

For some people, intellectual conversion is a serious and passionate project. The power of ideas and of whole systems of ideas is quite real to them. They subscribe to a particular philosophical school and apply its ideas to their lives in practical and meaningful ways. Plato and his student Aristotle, for example, disagreed fundamentally about how human experience should be interpreted, Plato being the idealist and Aristotle more the realist. Saint Augustine, in his long spiritual pilgrimage, investigated several of the popular philosophical schools of his time before choosing Christianity. Immanuel Kant spoke about his experience of awakening from a "dogmatic slumber," by which he meant an uncritical acceptance of the medieval philosophies he was taught as a youth; he then chose to develop his own philosophy. In more recent times we see scientific revolutions in which leading scientists break away from the accepted theory and offer a totally new way of interpreting the data.

Each of us can go through several such intellectual conversions in life. At our best, we consciously and intentionally adopt new ways of understanding and interpreting what we see in life, ways that help us sort out our experience. At the worst, we move with the crowd uncritically from one intellectual influence to another, not exercising our capacity to investigate why and how we change our assumptions.

Sometimes intellectual conversion seems more on a continuum, more a natural growth process as individual ideas lead from one to another until we discover that we have developed a significantly different way of thinking. At other times, the conversion is more a matter of discontinuity. We set aside a whole way of making sense of the world and substitute it with another. Perhaps our dissatisfaction with the old paradigm was brewing for a quite a while but we were not aware of it. Then when the convincing and challenging new set of ideas breaks into our awareness, we embrace it quickly and wholeheartedly. Sometimes it may take us the perspective afforded by years of subsequent experience to tell whether our intellectual conversion was more a matter of continuity or of discontinuity.

Moral Conversion

There is a second kind of conversion that we might call moral conversion. It is different from yet related to intellectual conversion. Moral conversion involves a significant, irrevocable, and radical shift in the way we prioritize our values. If strict justice and proper retribution were once our most highly prized virtues, but now we value compassion and mercy above all else, then we have undergone a moral conversion. If once our profession and work were the most important thing in our lives, and now it is our family, then we have undergone a moral conversion. If the acquisition of wealth and power was once the driving motivation in our lives, and now it is philanthropy and collaboration, then we have undergone a moral conversion. Moral conversion does not necessarily imply moral superiority. One can experience a shift in values and priorities and not live according to either the old or the new. As with intellectual conversion, one can change one's priorities simply because everyone else does as well. We can go through moral conversion because our whole society is shifting its priorities.

Sometimes it is an intellectual conversion that leads us to moral conversion. A different way of looking at life can result in a different way of living. Or our priorities may be shaken up and moved around because of the circumstances of our lives. In *Fiddler on the Roof*, Reb Tevye is a devout and devoted orthodox Jew whose life and opinions are arranged according to the Jewish law and customs. As his three daughters approach marriage, each strays more and more away from the expectations of their father and the accepted custom of his orthodox Jewish faith and culture. The first wants to marry without the matchmaker; the second to marry a revolutionary; the last to marry outside the faith. Tevye struggles with increasing angst over his daughters' choices as the priorities he was always taught and embraced are brought into question by their marriages. The marriage of his last daughter, however, seems to reconfirm his stance as an orthodox Jew. He shuns her rather than accept her decision to marry a gentile. At the very end of the story, however, he lets a paternal blessing go, with a sidelong glance in her direction. Reb Tevye seems to be on the brink of a moral conversion, of a reconsideration of how his religious convictions were to be interpreted and understood.

The ones we love, their decisions and needs, can force us to revisit our moral and ethical priorities. When a child we hold dear announces a sexual preference we think is sinful, the whole tower of our moral priorities can shake and fall. When a criminal is no longer an anonymous face on the front page of the newspaper, but someone we have known and loved, virtues and values get reexamined. When we ourselves face our own weakness and guilt honestly, then understanding and compassion can ascend our priority list to assume much higher relative places. In all such circumstances, when we are confronted with real life issues, we have to do the work of conscience. We have to reflect seriously on our moral assumptions. We need to consult others, to listen to those who have considered moral implications, and to hear out our religious traditions and the wisdom they might offer. The result of all this can be a moral conversion. It will not be an easy choice or change. Moral conversion is also a dying process. It will involve letting go, facing the unknown, and separation from what in the past has been a reliable guide.

Moral conversion is not moral agnosticism. It is not a giving up on value and virtue, a smashing of the moral compass. Moral conversion is not breaking down or giving up in the process of change. It is a coming through to a new and fuller and richer experience of virtue and value. It leads to a new way of making sense out of the complexities and ambiguities of motivation and purpose—our own and that of others.

Spiritual Conversion

A third type of conversion is spiritual conversion. Here the principal factor is not intellectual or moral. Certainly, intellect and morality can be and usually are important dimensions of religious conversions, part of a person's motivation for joining or changing religious affiliation. But spiritual conversion is not exactly the same as religious conversion. Spiritual conversion happens when we encounter the holy. It is not so much intellectual assent to a body of religious truth nor moral practice of ethical teachings. It is not even the habit of individual or communal prayer. Spiritual conversion happens when a person has the powerful experience of coming up against a power or a presence that he or she knows is totally above and beyond anything human. It is an encounter with the ultimate mystery, with the Holy of Holies, with God. It is a personally moving and even frightening—though not threatening—encounter. It is an awareness, new and startling, that there is a reality, wholly different and totally other, of immense, even infinite intensity, and that one dwells in and is surrounded by this presence. The experience may come all at once, unbidden and unexpected. Or it may grow slowly, imperceptibly, until it cannot be ignored. Spiritual conversion can be discontinuous, marking life before God and life since God. Or it can be more continuous, where the divine presence has slowly grown as part of one's life.

The sacred places and times of ancient peoples were surely associated with some type of spiritual conversions, of encounters with the holy. The sacred shrines and places of today's religions also mark the profound spiritual experience of some saint or prophet, and these places hold out the invitation to others that they, too, might there encounter the awesome presence and power of the divine. Spirituality as we have defined it is our relationship with God or the holy. Like all relationships, our relationship with God can be sometimes distant, sometimes close. It can be taken for granted or treasured. If we have had a spiritual conversion, a powerful and personal encounter with God, however, it cannot but permanently change and inform our spiritual life. It is a significant, irrevocable, and radical juncture along our spiritual journey.

Not everyone who practices a spiritual life will be able to identify one discrete and memorable moment when he or she felt face to face with God. Yet, unless spirituality is interpreted simply as a kind of practiced introspection, it must somehow take account of the reality of the holy, the presence of God in life. The spiritual life, with its practice of sacred time and place, is both a response to and an expectation of the divine presence. Sometimes that presence will be, as it was for Elijah the prophet, a tiny whisper; at other times it will approach like a tornado. A deeply felt experience of the holy, however, cannot fail to change our practice of the spiritual life. We can never enter our personal sacred space in the same way once the divine has entered our lives with the strength and power of a spiritual conversion experience.

A spiritual conversion is also a dying experience. Life before one's personal and immediate encounter with this divine mystery is part of a past that must be let go. Standing in the midst of an encounter with the holy is to stand before the completely and infinitely unknown one. And it is of the very essence of spiritual conversion that one is not in control. For at the very heart of such an encounter is the experience of surrender to the one who approaches. A spiritual conversion is a rising to new life. If one has been approached by the sacred, then everything changes. Everything takes on new meaning and significance. One is opened to whole new ways of experiencing and appropriating life.

Conversion and Hope

Hope is a virtue, a strength and conviction that enables us to turn toward the future with some measure of assurance and confidence. To be hopeless is to see no reason for moving ahead, no possibility of change or improvement. To be hopeful is not to dismiss the problems of the present nor the difficulties that are always awaiting us in the future. Hope is a willingness to move forward because our experience has taught us that things can improve and improve significantly.

Every type of conversion plants a seed of hope. The large and moving intellectual changes in our lives teach us that we can continue to learn. We can continue not only to learn new things, but learn new ways of learning and of thinking. Nothing breaks up a logjam of ideas like an explosive change in our intellectual assumptions and prejudices. Once that has happened to us, we know that it can happen again. While that knowledge can be disconcerting, it also inspires hope that whatever ideas and issues trouble us, there are wholly different ways of examining them that we have not yet learned.

Moral conversions are also signs of hope. The dilemmas and disappointments we are handed by our loved ones can become opportunities for rethinking what is really and truly important. Our own moral ambiguity and weakness can force us to reconsider our self-righteous stands and opinions. We can learn to live heuristically, always with an open mind and heart. To live that way is to live in hope.

Spiritual conversion is the ultimate source of hope. When we have despaired of finding God or any compelling meaning in life, when we feel that we live in endless exile, nothing so changes us as an encounter with the holy. That encounter may not answer any particular questions. It may not make our intellectual quest less difficult to pursue or our moral ambiguity much easier to sustain. But it gives us hope that we ourselves, our loved ones, and the world are all worth the effort.

CHAPTER 9

Commitment

Commitment is one of the greatest signs of hope. It inspires hope because it is an investment in the future. A commitment is made when someone who has studied the past and surveyed the present decides to affirm the future by accompanying someone into it. Commitment can also be made when a person decides to take an idea or a cause from the present into the future, confident that it can make that future better.

For a person who is in religious or spiritual exile, the question of commitment sooner or later comes up. If we no longer worship, if we demur at religious teachings, if we deny moral authority to religious leadership on certain issues, then are we still committed at some level to that faith or church? How firm was our commitment in the first place? If we remain within the institution, but quietly nurse doubts and misgivings within ourselves, have we compromised our commitment? Can a person lead a spiritual life without a commitment to a specific religious community or tradition? Does commitment differ from one religion to another? Can there be hope without commitment of some kind?

To begin to approach these and other questions about religious or spiritual commitment, it is helpful to discuss the various kinds of commitments we make in life. There are three basic types. We can commit ourselves to a person, to a community, or to a cause. This threefold distinction can help us understand the complexity of religious commitment and the subtleties of a faithful spiritual life.

Commitment in Personal Relationships

Among our romances, friendships, relations, and acquaintances, there are certain people to whom we are willing to commit ourselves. Romance can lead to the commitment of marriage. Friendships begun in youth or young adulthood can become lifelong when the parties make the necessary commitment of time and communication. The normal bonds of affection within our family or within our circle of acquaintances can be enhanced and confirmed when members strengthen and deepen their relationship with heartfelt commitment to one another. Yet there are many reasons we are drawn more powerfully to this or that particular person. Before we make commitments, it is helpful and instructive to ask why we are doing it, especially since commitment carries significant consequences.

Into every relationship we carry a bag of needs. Early in a relationship the bag is usually well hidden, or at least its contents are kept inside. Some of these needs are what may be called normal healthy needs. Into our romances we take the need to be loved particularly, to be held and soothed, to be loved physically and sexually. Into our friendships we carry the need to share confidences, to be mirrored and idealized, to be set apart together from the crowd. Among our family members we gravitate toward those who see things in the family as we do, who share our memories and interpretations of our common past, who have similar hopes and dreams for the future. Even our daily acquaintances at work or play meet our needs for easy companionship and conversation. An awareness of these needs is important. When we are as clear as we can be about our expectations of the friend or spouse, of the sibling or acquaintance, then communication is easier and mutual understanding grows.

We can also bring a different type of need into relationships. This kind of need could be called unhealthy or neurotic. If what motivates our behavior toward the other is an unconscious need for endless acceptance and affirmation, the relationship will soon become stressed. If you are the object of such narcissistic need, you will feel like you are in a relationship with an octopus whose psychological tentacles have you covered and restrict your every movement.

In romance, friendship, and other relationships, this type of unhealthy, neurotic need can counterfeit as commitment. Excessive need of another person, obsessive demands on another's time and interest, can at first look like commitment. But its motivation is mixed at best. The very needy person is committed; but it is a one way commitment to relief from the persistent deep anxiety around his or her worth and value. The beloved or the friend is objectified as a means to that end. Such possessiveness is not commitment.

True commitment does not require that we purge ourselves of all needs. That is impossible. We all persist in our neediness to some extent. What commitment does require, however, is some degree of *agape,* some measure of unconditional and freely given love for the other. Only God's love is pure *agape.* Our human loves are always a mixture of need and gift, of being taken care of and generously taking care, of receiving and giving. Commitment assesses one's own needs as well as the needs of the beloved or the friend. It also takes account of each other's capacity for *agape* and willingness to love freely, without reservation or even expectation. Then it decides to walk with that person into the future side by side, agreeing to continue to negotiate needs and celebrate gifts. Commitment is an act of will. It is a deliberate decision that acknowledges as many levels of motivation as one can discern, and yet affirms one's own and the other's capacity to make this act of will on each other's behalf.

Commitment is never without risk. There is no guarantee that spouse or child, good friend, or blood brother or sister will always be there and will never fail to love us unconditionally. This lack of certainty frightens many away from commitment. Yet all we have about the reliability of relationships and the trustworthiness of others is what might be called "certitude." *Certainty* is objective assurance or ironclad insurance about the future behaviors of ourselves or of others. It is the desire for a contract that stipulates in detail what will happen between you and the one to whom you are to commit. *Certitude,* on the other hand, is a subjective conviction about the other person's motivation. It is a covenant, a pledge to remain faithful and responsive as you both change and grow throughout the years. Commitment grows out of certitude. It can never arise from certainty.

We can grow in our relationships. We can become more and more aware of our own needs and how we expect the other to meet them. We can come to understand with increasing clarity what the other needs from us. We can also learn that our different needs change and develop. We may even find that our love helps to heal the beloved's neurotic need, or that our own narcissistic wounds can be touched and healed by the *agape* we receive from the beloved or the friend. It is in the midst of these revelations and disclosures that the ongoing possibility of commitment arises. When it does, and when we act upon it, the relationship is transformed and carried into the future, and we become a source of hope for our beloved, our friends, and our acquaintances, even as we receive hope as a gift from them.

Commitment to Causes and Communities

We can also make commitments to causes and communities. A cause may be political, such as one's nation and homeland or a particular political ideology. We may also make a lifelong commitment to artistic endeavor or to a religion. In almost all such cases there is a community of persons associated with or gathered around the cause that we find so compelling. Commitment to the cause will often involve commitment to the community that surrounds and embraces it.

As with commitment to another person, commitment to a cause or community is an affirmation that promises to bring the idea into the future, to ensure that the community that surrounds the cause does not die out. The value and importance we ascribe to the idea or value involved is so strong that our time, energy, effort, and talent are all dedicated to advance it. Such lifelong commitment can sometimes be made even to the exclusion of many other possible life choices, including the personal commitment of marriage.

The complex kinds of motivations in commitments to other persons are also to be found in commitments to causes and communities. We often become part of movements and associations simply because they satisfy our need to belong. We want to do something meaningful, to be part of something that is bigger than ourselves and that will outlast us in history. We can support causes and join communities because our involvement gets recognition and affirmation that we need. If our needs are stronger than our belief in the project, we can end up doing more that gets in the way of the cause than actually helps it.

Or, our motivation may be more selfless. We want to give coming generations an idea, a philosophy, a conviction that we believe will better their lives and their society. As with commitment to persons, we will never totally divest ourselves of self-interest. However, if we can move beyond the sole motivation of personal payback, it is helpful. There is great value in becoming as reflective as we can about our motivations for being involved in a cause or a community. The more aware we are about what moves and inspires us to such commitment, the freer we are to serve that cause.

Causes and communities, like individuals, can also disappoint us. On one level, they may end up not meeting our needs, even our healthy, normal needs to belong and be part of something of value and purpose. At another level, they may fail to satisfy our unhealthy, neurotic needs and leave us bitter and resentful. In either case, when a person has dedicated a whole life and committed his or her whole being to a cause or community, much is on the line. There are no guarantees when we make such commitments. As is the case with relationships, we do not ever have certainty about a cause or a community. What we can have is certitude, an inner conviction and belief that the principles behind the movement or the community are of such vital importance and essential value for culture and society that we make the dedication of our life to advance them.

In personal relationships symbols become very important to express and celebrate the commitment people have made to one another. A wedding ring, a gift that symbolizes a cherished friendship, a photo of a special family member—we constantly and instinctively look for ways to express the importance and meaning that our committed relationships have. Indeed, such symbolic expressions are essential for the commitment to continue and deepen over the years.

Causes and communities also need symbols that convey and articulate their meaning and message. When one has committed to a movement or organization, its symbols take on great importance. They become expressions of personal allegiance, affection, and loyalty. One's ongoing commitment to the group is expressed not only through work and action, but also through celebrating and cherishing the group's symbols. This is an especially important dimension when the cause and community is of a religious or spiritual nature.

Commitment and Faith

What we customarily call religious faith is commitment to both a cause and a community. The cause is what the religion teaches about the interpretation and meaning of life and creation, and what it advises and expects about ethical behavior and right choices. The community is the group of people who embrace the teaching now and who have embraced it throughout the history of the religious group.

Commitment to religious faith can be quite complex; it is not a simple, one-category reality. There are at least three major dimensions of religious faith we can investigate here. This is not an exhaustive study, but it does begin to show how to approach the complexity of faith. We can use the same categories from our consideration of conversion: namely, intellectual, moral, and spiritual. Each of these categories enables us to approach religious faith and personal commitment to faith from a different perspective.

The intellectual dimension of faith concerns the teachings, the doctrines, or dogmas of the religion. These teachings are about the nature of God, about what God may have revealed or spoken through prophets or saints, about the meaning of creation and our role in it as human beings. Some religions are more doctrinal than others. Christianity, for example, is rich in doctrines that members are expected to believe and support. Some of the major Christian doctrines are that Jesus is the Son of God, that the nature of God is triune, that all creation comes from God, that salvation comes through Christ, and so forth. Judaism, on the other hand, is not a doctrinal religion. Jews are defined and confirmed by their observance and interpretation of the Law of Moses, rather than by assent to religious dogma.

So in some religions more than others, faith involves intellectual assent to revealed teachings. The faithful Christian believer makes a commitment on an intellectual level to the doctrines of the church. It is a commitment to a cause, the "cause" of Jesus of Nazareth, if you will. And it is a commitment to a community, to those who also profess faith in Jesus as Lord and in his teachings. It is not a commitment without risk. As with any cause or any person, there is no certainty, only certitude. The power of religious faith is not to be found in the unassailable facts that it guarantees or in any kind of contract that one signs. The value of religious faith is to be sought in the certitude that the believer celebrates in union with other believers. Intellectual faith is not the same as tight logic or empirical proof. Intellectual faith is affirmation that these teachings, in the light of which the believer lives, are able to unlock meaning and purpose more effectively and more convincingly than any others.

Faith also involves moral commitment. Religions usually counsel a set of commandments or observances. The believer is expected to commit to these moral precepts by living in accordance with them. Judaism, as we have seen, is defined more by its moral precepts than its doctrine. The Torah provides guidance for all aspects of life. Christianity and Islam build on the moral traditions of the Hebrew scriptures and also offer their adherents moral systems by which to abide.

The moral precepts of a religion are ideally embodied in the community of believers. The believer's willingness to live by these precepts is a fundamental way of living out one's commitment to the community. Here, too, there is risk. There is no guarantee that the community will itself be faithful to those same precepts, or that the individual believer will always be treated in light of a particular religion's stated morality. Again, on this level of moral commitment, there is not certainty—only certitude that the moral teachings are in and of themselves compelling, liberating, and humanizing.

There is a third and equally important level of commitment in religious faith. This is the spiritual level. Spiritual conversion is an encounter with the presence and power of the holy in our life. Spiritual commitment in religious faith is our personal response to that encounter. It is a humble and joyful recognition of the divine who has approached and invited the believer into relationship. Commitment at this level involves the spiritual life. If we believe that God has come into our life personally and powerfully, then living our life in light of that encounter is an expression of commitment. Making frequent pilgrimages to our sacred space is a way of remembering and celebrating that personal encounter with the holy. In fact, one's sacred time and place are continuing opportunities for loving dialogue with the holy. In the quiet and hospitable interiority of sacred space, one can watch and wait for the presence of the divine. Of course, as with doctrine and moral precept, there is no certainty about spiritual commitment. However, those who have had powerful encounters with the holy, whose lives have been changed and redirected because of an experience of the divine presence and power, have sufficient certitude to make a spiritual commitment and to live spiritual lives.

In the Christian faith, the believer's personal commitment to Jesus is a key dimension of spiritual commitment. For the Christian, the Holy One is revealed in and through Jesus. The felt experience of Christian faith is of having been approached by Christ, of having encountered the Risen Lord. One's spiritual life, therefore, is lived in union with Christ, in ongoing, loving commitment to and with him.

Religious symbols express the many aspects of faith commitment. On one level, they give palpable form and shape to doctrinal teachings. In art and sculpture the teachings of many religions find expression that can be more powerful and attractive than simple words. At another level, stories about the courage of saints, martyrs, and prophets illustrate moral teachings and give them a powerful and lasting impression. At the level of the soul, the poetry and music expressing a mystic's encounter with the holy invites others to consider the possibility of such revelation in their own lives. Such symbols can capture more than one level of religious commitment at the same time. A hymn can teach doctrine through its lyrics while capturing religious sentiment in its melody and harmonies. An icon can teach about dogma even as it invites the worshiper into the very presence of the Holy One. Religious symbols become ways for those who have made a commitment in faith to renew their commitment and deepen it in so doing.

There are times in the lives of all believers when one aspect of faith is stronger or more important than others. Sometimes the doctrines are of vital import and meaning. At other times moral precepts and the challenge they present to us become paramount. At still other times, our personal encounter with God is the most keenly felt dimension of our faith. At such times the Christian's personal relationship with Jesus, the Jew's mystical experience of the holy, the Muslim's profound and liberating submission to Allah sustains and gives meaning to all other aspects of one's religious faith.

There are also times when one or more levels of faith are difficult, even for the committed believer. One might doubt certain doctrines but remain morally observant and faithful. Or intellectual and spiritual commitment may be strong, while one struggles with one or another moral precept of the faith. At other times moral life and spiritual encounter may make intellectual assent to doctrine seem of little meaning or purpose. And there are times when doctrine and morality must subsist on their own because any personal experience of the divine presence is a memory from long ago. A life of faith commitment, however, is lived on these three intertwining levels. It is a life not without risk, and one that does indeed call for constant recommitment.

Spirituality and Faith Commitment

A question that arises frequently today is whether or not one can be spiritual without being religious. Can one live a spiritual life without making any kind of commitment to a particular religious faith and community? The reverse of this question is also pertinent. Can one live a life of committed faith without being spiritual?

Regarding the latter question, we have seen that even committed religious believers may go for long periods in their lives without any felt spiritual encounter with the holy. The devout and observant believer may not have any strong spiritual or mystical experiences, yet still remain committed in faith. One would not call them unspiritual. They can maintain a faithful commitment to the spiritual life, even to daily pilgrimage, living patiently and expectantly in the quiet of their souls.

On the other hand, there are members of religions whose participation is less a matter of commitment and more an inherited circumstance. They may have been born into a particular religion, or joined it for social, cultural, or even business reasons. They may have some appreciation of doctrine and at least nominal assent to moral precept. There has been, however, no deeper faith commitment. Such persons have the external accoutrements of religion but not the interiority of spirituality. In such cases there is a kind of religious affiliation without any spirituality.

What of the opposite? Can there be a deep and abiding spirituality in the life of a person who has severed relationship with organized religion, or who never belonged to one in the first place? Can a person who eschews faith commitment live the spiritual life, live in ways that work relationship with the holy into the fabric of daily life? Is it possible that some people need the distance from religion as they know it in order to live a spiritual life? It seems there are indeed deeply spiritual people who do not live in any kind of committed relationship to a specific religious tradition or community of faith. However, a simple Yes or No answer to this question about spirituality and religious faith ignores the complex issues in both religious faith and the spiritual life.

To begin with, spirituality and the spiritual life are not static. At one point in life a person who has been alienated from organized, traditional religion may find a deep and abiding spirituality only in his or her religious exile. To such a person God may be more real in the desert than in the church or temple. As one makes a commitment to the spiritual life and begins to live it day in and day out, however, questions inevitably arise. In the quiet hospitality of one's sacred place, questions will begin to emerge about the nature of this God, this Holy One who means so much and brings such joy and consolation in the spiritual desert. They may not exactly be questions of fine dogmatic points, but they may well involve doctrinal or theological issues. Unless a person works very hard to keep mind and heart apart, questions about the nature of God will eventually present themselves during the spiritual pilgrimage.

For a person who was raised in a particular religious tradition, these questions are usually formed and informed by the religious and doctrinal language that they learned growing up. A person's religious background will assert itself in these musings on God and on other mysteries of the transcendent. This is not necessarily a drawback, even for the believer who has been displaced for severe and painful reasons. In fact, in the solitude and quiet of the desert, a person may actually begin to hear and understand the old religious language in new and refreshing ways. One might find in the old words valuable insights into one's present spiritual experience.

A truly spiritual person will also strive to be diligent. So questions about how to live a diligent life will present themselves. Curiosity about how to connect one's spirituality with morality will lead to ethical questions. Here again the religious and moral language learned during religious upbringing will more often than not assert itself into later ethical queries.

Spirituality cannot be isolated from intellect and will unless one wishes to relegate it to the realm of sentiment. The spiritual life engages our hearts and our minds as well as our souls. By nature we strive to connect the different parts of our lives and weave them into meaningful patterns. To put it in other words, spirituality naturally seeks a theology and a morality. The spiritual life will constantly tend toward religious questions about the divine and about living with loving care and hope. It will continually seek language in which to frame and pursue these questions. More often than not, the religious language we learned growing up in a particular religious tradition will supply the categories and images for the intellectual and moral dimensions of our spiritual life. We may also search among the wisdom and literature of other religious traditions for help in formulating such questions, but our first religious language will usually maintain its strong cognitive influence.

Most people who remain spiritual pilgrims for a long time find that they do in fact develop in their understanding of God, of the mystery of the Holy One. They also are intentionally reflective about their moral values and priorities. Very often their personal theologies and moralities are remarkably similar to those of traditional religion, even of the religion to which they may once have belonged. The more poignant question for the displaced believer who lives the spiritual life is whether or not eventually to make a commitment to cause and community. Spiritual pilgrims, once alienated from religion, may have difficulty expressing or making a commitment to any particular religious institution, cause, or ideology. They may also have difficulty committing to the institution as a community of persons who affirm and embrace particular religious doctrine and morality. Such hesitation must be respected. The difficulty for such displaced believers has not come out of thin air; the institutional religion or members of the religious community may be complicit in the difficulty.

Yet the spiritual life is already a commitment in and of itself. The spiritual pilgrim commits to the journey, to the inner excavation, to the quest for understanding. Whatever image or metaphor one uses to understand and explain the spiritual life, there is movement toward a goal to which one is in fact committed. Otherwise we should speak of the spiritual life as a vacation rather than a pilgrimage, as tunneling to nowhere rather than a careful excavation, as an exercise in rhetoric rather than a passionate search for truth.

For some pilgrims the spiritual journey will mean an eventual return to the religion they once knew well. As we have already discussed, such a return will not be an easy or simple journey. For others, the spiritual life will mean commitment to a new religion that more closely reflects the sacred as they have come to experience it. For still others, the commitment of the spiritual life will be lived in permanent exile from organized religion and religious tradition. Yet this exile does not have to mean exclusion from spiritual friendships with committed believers who live their spiritual lives within particular religious traditions. In such friendships between the committed believer and the religious exile there is already a commitment to each other. In reality, spiritual friendships shared among several persons of differing religious persuasions already constitute a spiritual community and a commitment to that community. Their commitment to each other affirms the value of interiority and of the sacred for humankind, and a readiness to support each other in taking that conviction into the future. Such commitment to spiritual friendship is a sign of hope for all who treasure the spiritual life and who value religious questions.

Commitment and Hope

So there is one commitment that can inspire hope to all those who choose to live a diligent, spiritual life. It is this commitment to one another in a society of spiritual friendship. The believer who is deeply committed to an ancient and venerable religious tradition can find in the more solitary spiritual pilgrim a companion for at least some of the journey of faith. Such companionship can lead each to consider how the spiritual life is lived in another way. Those who find they cannot nurture their souls in organized religion may find the more hospitable members of such religions to be faithful and loving spiritual companions. Insights may come in unexpected ways from unexpected quarters. Believers who come from different religious faiths can find in each other spiritual companions, even soul mates. One can learn to appreciate a different perspective from which another approaches the holy.

Such relationships are occasions of grace. The Holy One can reach out to us, approach us, and embrace us through those who share our spiritual hunger, if not our religious taste. We can receive insight and revelation, consolation and comfort, encouragement and enlightenment from the motley crowd of our spiritual companions. To meet and talk with others who value interiority can help us appreciate our own inner lives all the more. To welcome into our sacred space others whose backgrounds or religious convictions are very different from our own is to receive a great blessing. To dwell in quiet, without words and other distractions, with those who also desire the sacred silence is a great joy. To share the diligent life in friendship and love with other spiritual pilgrims is a source and a sign of immense hope for our world and for those who will inherit it from us.

Postscript

This text may have met you at any number of places along the journey. You may have found it alongside the dusty, dry track of a bleak and lonely spiritual exile. My hope is that it has supplied you some resources and refreshment to ease that exile. Or you may have found it as you are leaving the religious tradition that was once your home. In that case, the ideas discussed here might encourage you to make of your uncertain journey a spiritual pilgrimage. Still another possibility is that you are searching for a way to return to religious faith and commitment. Perhaps these pages might serve to guide your return, to help make it more intentional and informed. Some readers will bring this text into their faith commitment and faith community. I hope it enriches both. And there will be those whose way is much more uncertain, whose maps are confusing, whose spiritual life is agnostic. To you this text is an offer of spiritual friendship.

From where you are on your life's journey, you may see things differently than these pages describe. You may propose different understandings of the spiritual life, of love and care, of grace and hope, understandings that express your own experience and reflection. Your response and insight is critical to the message and intent of this text. Your take on religious and spiritual exile is just as important and perhaps more astute than the one described here. You need to accept and embrace, to care for and cherish your own understandings. You need to bring them to your reading and possibly to the conversations on spirituality that may arise with those you meet along the way.

In these pages I have drawn from the wisdom of several religious traditions. My own life and faith journey have been enriched by the gracious presence and spiritual friendship of religious pilgrims from other religious traditions. Yet it has been the person and preaching of Jesus that have ultimately led me along the way, opened me to truth, and guided my life. My faith in Christ and in the gift of the Spirit lead me to affirm God's presence and power in the spiritual friendship that we share as writer and reader.

In the exchange between you and this text, the very process of divine creation continues. In the sacred time and place where our ideas meet, the Holy One once again breathes the Divine Spirit over our conversation and new possibilities emerge. Our dialogue about exile and the spiritual life will enrich not only us; it will also give hope to others. Our mutual loving care for the many ways in which the spiritual life might be lived will help to make our world more hospitable and sustaining for those who are to follow us along the pilgrim path.